Beer
B A S I C S

Peter LaFrance

BEER

B A S I C S

A
Quick
AND
Easy
Guide

JOHN WILEY & SONS, INC.
New York | Chichester | Brisbane | Toronto | Singapore

Library of Congress Cataloging-in-Publication Data
LaFrance, Peter
    Beer basics : a quick and easy guide / Peter LaFrance
       p.   cm.
    Includes bibliographic references and index.
    ISBN 0-471-11936-9 (pbk. : acid-free)
    1. Beer. I. Title
  TP577.L33 1995
  641.2′3—dc   94-49717

Printed in the United States of America

10 9 8 7 6 5 4 3 2 1

To my wife, Virginia, and daughter, Mary

CONTENTS

Preface

This book is for those who are interested in finding out about the basics of beer appreciation. If you picked this book up by mistake because it was right next to a new guide to Bordeaux, there is something here for you too. Is this universal welcome unsettling? Let me offer the following anecdote.

A few years ago I was enjoying a conversation with a number of people at a beer event. During the conversation, Fritz Maytag, the president of Anchor Brewing Company, and I began comparing the appreciation of beer with the appreciation of wine. One of the members of our group became alarmed that we had wandered off the "proper" conversational path. Maytag's response was simple and to the point: "We are all friends in fermentation."

In that spirit, pun intended, welcome to the world of beer. You are about to embark on a fascinating journey—the appreciation and enjoyment of beer, not only as a refreshing beverage, but an essential accompaniment to good food, good friends, and good conversation.

Now to the matter at hand. My aim is to introduce you to the essentials of beer. This book will concentrate on what goes into beer, present an overview of the brewing process, and acquaint you with the vocabulary of beer appreciation. This book is an introduction to the fascinating world of lagers, ales, porters, and many other tasty brews.

First you will learn about the basic ingredients and the process of brewing beer. Then you will read a short history of brewing before you are introduced to the different styles of beers and their distinctive personalities. Finally, you will have a chance to discover how much fun it is to match the unique personalities of your favorite beers with your favorite foods.

Most important, this book is indexed and cross-indexed so that you have ready access to information rather than having to search through passages in which you have no particular interest at any particular moment.

P.S. This book has been written primarily for North American readers, especially those in the United States. The beers that are featured in this book, unless otherwise noted, are sold in retail shops in most of the United States. If you cannot find a particular beer mentioned in this book, check with your retailer, or their wholesaler, and ask for it. You might be surprised what happens.

Acknowledgments

I would like to thank the following people who made this book possible: my sister Linda LaFrance, who set the wheels in motion; Kim Hendrickson, for her guidance; and Claire Thompson, for her faith in me.

The following people were invaluable in gathering and developing the material in this book: Kate Begley, Jane Chamberlain, Linda Dilworth, Steve Harrison, Susan Henderson, Michael Hennick, Michelle C. Kliner, Wendy Littlefield, Wendy May, Ian McAllister, James Munson, Casey W. Raskob, Carol A. Stoudt, Keith Symonds, Jim Woodcock, and Patti Zenk; Chef John Doherty, Chef Billy Hahn, Chef Benito Malivert, Chef Rick Moonen, Chef Michel Notredame, and Marc Kadish.

Special thanks to the management and staffs of the Broome Street Bar and of Nick and Eddie in New York City.

BEER
BASICS

Introduction

In 1978 there were 89 breweries in operation in the United States, producing fewer than 25 nationally distributed brands. Today there are more than 400 breweries, producing more than 1,000 different beers. There are more different styles of beer produced in the United States than in any other country in the world. How did all this happen in less than 20 years?

As Fritz Maytag (Anchor Brewing Company) said, "We are all friends in fermentation," and so it was in California in the mid-1960s. People with money, and with an appreciation of fine wine, began investing in California real estate, developing vineyards. They envisioned a time when California would become another Bordeaux. They invested, they planted, and they waited. The vines grew and produced fine grapes, the weather was predictable, and then the Internal Revenue Service revised the "Limited Partnership" provisions that made investing in ventures like cattle futures and boutique wineries so profitable. Today, even with the shakeout of financially distressed wineries, there is a good amount of world-class wine flowing from the Napa, Sonoma, and Mendicino valleys of California. The success of the wineries caught the attention of other entrepreneurs. These were people who knew what well-made, fresh beer tasted like. It was a demand waiting to be satisfied.

It happened in 1977, in Sonoma, California. That was the year the first United States "micro brewery," the New Albion Brewing Company (annual production, 200 barrels), began producing a British-style ale and a stout. Its market was limited, but its reputation flourished in the friendly climate of the California wine country.

In fact, import beers were beginning to find increasing favor with consumers who were returning from their travels overseas and demanding the same full-flavored beers they had enjoyed in Europe. These consumers insisted on foods and beverages of quality, and they knew what quality was. It meant knowing what went into a product, not what brand name was on it. This search for quality continues unabated.

Today the world of beer has never been more exciting. Fine restaurants feature "beer-tasting menus," similar to traditional wine-tasting menus. New beers are coming on the market every week. Even the major brewing companies are now introducing products with more flavor to cater to the market segment that usually purchases imported or domestic "specialty" beers. If the big boys are willing to make major changes in their products and advertising campaigns, the trend of a few years ago is now a full-fledged market segment.

My basic intention in writing this book is to provide a guide to the styles of beers now available in the United States, rather than simply announce a selection of beers that I find interesting and leave you wondering why that "awful-tasting" gueuze is considered a classic style of beer.

I hope you will have many pleasant opportunities to use this guide as you explore the world of beer. More to the point, please share what you discover with family, friends, and acquaintances. To that end I offer this toast—To your health!

WHO GETS MENTIONED?

As this is a book on "basics," I must limit the selection of beers mentioned to products that are in nationwide distribution in the United States. However, because of their historical significance, importance to the development of a "style," or contribution to the general world of beer and brewing, I have included some esoteric selections, especially the monastic Abby and Trappist breweries of Belgium. (All beers that are not available nationwide are followed by asterisks.)

ASK FOR IT!

If you are really interested in enjoying good beer, you are going to have to start asking for it. Write or fax the producing brewery and ask if there are plans to begin sales in your area. Amazing things happen when customers ask for products with which a business owner can make a high profit margin.

CHAPTER ONE
WHAT IS BEER?

Quite simply, beer is fermented, hop-flavored, malt sugar tea. There are four basic building blocks needed to make beer: **water, malted barley, hops,** and **yeast.** Yeast, listed as a fourth ingredient, is used to ferment the hop-flavored malt sugar tea into an effervescent liquid with an average of between 3% and 7% ethyl alcohol by weight. (In some cases, such as in a barleywine, the alcohol content can go to almost 11% by weight.) Both beer and ale are made from essentially the same four building blocks, with the major variation being the type of yeast used to ferment the product. The following is a brief description of the four important building blocks of beer.

WATER

Water comprises more than 90% of beer. In the past, the mineral content of natural springs or artesian wells constituted a major flavor factor in the beers that were produced in a specific region. Examples of naturally occurring water supplies that have resulted in distinctive beer styles are found at Burton-on-Trent in the United Kingdom (Bass Ale) and Esopus in New York State.

Today, brew masters can chemically adjust any water to create the exact "style" of beer desired. The chemicals added to the water are most often mineral salts such as gypsum or Epsom salts.

These salts cause the hop oils to develop specific, pronounced flavor characteristics that enhance their use as flavoring agents.

Although the phrase "pure water" has been used extensively in advertisements for beers and ales, every brewery carefully adjusts the water it uses to meet its specific flavor profile.

MALTED BARLEY

Barley, a basic cereal grain, is low in gluten and not particularly good for milling into flour for use in products such as bread or bakery goods that need gluten, in concert with yeast, to work. There are three major types of barley. Each is differentiated by the number of seeds that grow at the top of the stalk. Barley seeds grow in two, four, and six rows, along a central stem. European brewers prefer two-row barley because it malts best and has a better starch/husk ratio than four- or six-row barley. Brewers in the United States prefer the six-row barley because it is more economical to grow and has a higher concentration of the enzymes needed to convert the starch in the grain into sugar and other fermentables. The barley grains must be "malted" before they can be used in the brewing process.

Malting is a process of bringing grain to the point of its highest possible soluble starch content, by allowing it to begin to sprout roots and take the first step to becoming a photosynthesizing plant. At this point the seed is rich in the starch it needs to use as food for growth.

When the maximum starch content is reached, the maltster heats the grain to a temperature that stops the growth process but allows an important natural enzyme, diastase (which converts starch into sugar), to remain active. Barley, once malted is very high in the type of starches that diastase (found naturally on the surface of the grain, just under the husk) can convert quite easily into a rich sugar called maltose. This sugar is metabolized by the ale or lager yeast to create carbon dioxide (CO_2) and ethyl alcohol.

Portions of this malted barley are then heated at higher temperatures to "roast" it. The roasted malted barley no longer has the active enzymes needed to turn the starches into sugars, but it does take on characteristics that add to the flavor of the beer. The degree of roasting results in malted barley that ranges from light tan (Dortmund and Bavarian), to "patent" and "chocolate" malt (roasted until almost black). These roasted malts add flavor and color to both ales and lager-style beer.

HOPS

The hop (*humulus lupulus*) is a flowering vine. In the brewing process, the flowers of the hop vine are used for their preservative value and for essential oils that add flavor and aroma to balance the sweetness of the malt used in the beer.

The hop plant is a perennial spiraling vine that can grow to climb string or poles to heights of more than 25 feet. The flowers (or cones as they are sometimes called) are usually dried before use. The bitter flavor is extracted from the hops during the boil. It is during this time that virtually insoluble alpha acids are isomerized (rearranged without changing their composition) into more soluble and stable iso-alpha acids, the main bittering substance in beer.

Hops bring a lot more to beer than bitterness. Brewers seek to maximize hop flavor and aroma with high-quality "aroma" hops. The essential oils are what give hops their unique aroma; each variety has its own distinct profile.

Dry-hopping, the addition of hops to the secondary fermenter or serving tank, is another way to add hop character to a beer although the aroma components retained by this method differ from those obtained in late kettle additions.

Researchers have not been able to duplicate the complexities of hoppy character by adding pure chemicals in any proportion or combination. Consensus is that there is a synergistic blend of several compounds, some of which may have not yet been discovered. Hop researchers, using capillary gas chromatography, have detected and identified more than 250 essential oil components in hops. Twenty-two of these have been pinpointed as being good indicators of hoppiness potential.

Following is a list of the most well-known hops—where they are grown, their flavor profiles, and examples of the beers that use each.

Cascade is grown in the United States and has a floral, citrus (grapefruit) aroma. It is used for bittering, finishing, and dry-hopping American-style ales such as Sierra Nevada Pale Ale, Anchor Liberty Ale, and Old Foghorn.

East Kent Goldings is grown in the United Kingdom and has a spicy/floral flavor with an earthy, almost pungent aroma. It is used for bittering, finishing, and dry-hopping British-style ales such as Young's Special London Ale, Samuel Smith's Pale Ale, and Fuller's ESB.

Fuggles is grown both in the United Kingdom and in the United States. It has a mild, soft, floral aroma. Fuggles is used for finishing and dry-hopping ales and dark lagers such as Samuel Smith's Pale Ale, Old Peculier, and Thomas Hardy's Ale.

Hallertauer Mittelfrueh is grown in Germany and has a pleasant, spicy, mild herbal aroma. It is used for finishing

German-style lagers such as Sam Adams Boston Lager and Sam Adams Boston Lightship.

Saaz is grown both in the Czech and Slovak Republics. It has a delicate, mild, floral aroma and is used primarily as a finishing hop in Bohemian-style lagers such as Pilsner Urquell.

Tettnang is grown both in Germany and in the United States. Tettnang has a fine, very spicy aroma and is used in finishing German-style lagers such as Gulpener Pilsener, Sam Adams Octoberfest, and Anderson Valley ESB.

YEAST

Yeast are unicellular fungi. Most brewing yeasts belong to the genus *Saccharomyces.* Ale yeast are *S. cerevisiae,* and lager yeast are *S. uvarum* (formerly *carlsbergerensis*).

Although the principal tastes present in beer are the result of the malts and hops used, the strain of yeast used also adds flavor. Yeast that add little in the way of extra flavors are usually described as having a "clean" taste. Yeast produce three metabolic by-products that affect beer taste: phenols, ester, and diacetyl. Phenols can give a spicy or clove-like taste or a medicinal taste. Esters lend a fruity taste to beer. Diacetyls have a butterscotch or sometimes a "woody" taste. The desirability of any one of these components depends largely on the style of the beer being brewed. A lot depends on the individual palate and the effect the brewer is aiming for.

During fermentation, the normal temperatures for ale yeast range from 60 to 75°F (16 to 24°C). Lager strains normally ferment from 32 to 75°F (0 to 24°C). The average fermentation time for ale yeast is 7–8 days. Lager fermentation often takes as much as a month.

ADJUNCTS

Adjuncts are anything other than malted barley, hops, water, and yeast used in the brewing or fermentation of beer. Among the most commonly used adjuncts are corn, rice, and sugar. The federal and state agencies that regulate the content of foods and beverages also allow brewers to use over 200 chemical additives. Adjuncts are used to produce less expensive beer with an extensive shelf life.

CHAPTER TWO

How Beer Is Made

Beer (both lager and ale) is made in a brew house. A brew house consists of a grist mill, mash tun, copper, fermenter, fermenting tanks, conditioning tanks, and usually a kegging or bottling line. In the case of a brew pub there is no bottling or kegging, so the beer is drawn to the tap directly from the conditioning tanks. The traditional brewery (building containing a brew house) was built on at least three levels. This was done to allow gravity to do much of the work of moving the grain, grist, mash, wort, and spent grains. It was also important that the fermenting and conditioning tanks be in cellars where the temperature was optimum for the fermenting and conditioning of the beer. Ale can be fermented and conditioned at a higher temperature than lager, but both need cool, stable temperatures to produce the best product.

GRIST

The first step is to crush the grain into grist. The grain is rolled between metal rollers that are set a specific distance apart so that the crushing is done without turning the grain into flour. The grain should be crushed just enough to allow for optimum extraction of the fermentable sugars when hot water/"liquor" is added to create the "mash."

THE MASH

The easiest brewing process begins when the crushed grain (grist) is shoveled into the mash tun where hot "liquor" (*see* page 180) (water), heated to approximately 175°F, is added. This is the "striking" temperature, which is a few degrees higher than the optimum mash temperature of about 150 to 152°F. However, this is the best temperature for the enzymes found naturally in the grain to turn the starches, which make up most of the grain into fermentable sugars, which are fermented by the yeast later in the process.

The temperature range of the mash creates the optimum environment for the enzymes to convert the soluble starches in the malted barley into sugar and other nonfermentable products. Lower temperatures usually produce more nonfermentables; higher temperatures mean fewer nonfermentable products. These nonfermentables give the finished beer "body," or "mouth feel."

THE BOIL/BREW

At this point the sweet liquor, now called "wort," is piped into a kettle where it is boiled with the hops until the proteins are precipitated from the wort and the essential oils are extracted from the hops. The hopped wort is then quickly chilled to about 60°F and piped into fermenting tanks.

FERMENTATION

The fermenting tanks are filled with the cool wort, and then either top-fermenting or bottom-fermenting yeast is "pitched" (added) and fermentation takes place. Basically, this is when

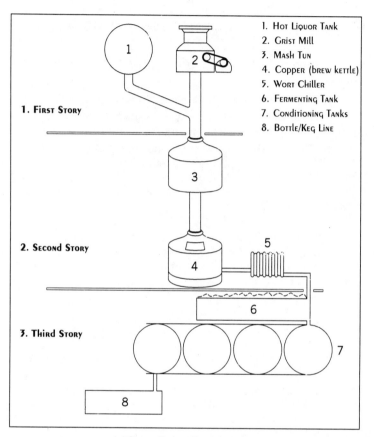

1. Hot Liquor Tank
2. Grist Mill
3. Mash Tun
4. Copper (brew kettle)
5. Wort Chiller
6. Fermenting Tank
7. Conditioning Tanks
8. Bottle/Keg Line

1. First Story

2. Second Story

3. Third Story

A Three-Story Brew House

the yeast metabolizes the sugar in the wort, and the resulting products are ethyl alcohol and carbon dioxide.

CARBONATION/FINISHING

When almost all the fermentable sugar has been changed into ethyl alcohol and CO_2, the brew is piped into special "finishing tanks" where the yeast is allowed to finishing fermenting. These fermentation tanks are designed to withstand the pressure created as the yeast produces the CO_2 necessary for effervescence in the beer.

In some commercial mass-production breweries this step is bypassed and the fermented brew is injected with CO_2. This process is much faster than "natural" conditioning.

The brew is then bottled, kegged, or, in the case of pub breweries, drawn by taps in the bar and served to customers.

CHAPTER
THREE
A Short History
of Beer

PREHISTORIC BEER

There is some debate as to whether grain was first cultivated specifically for use in brewing beer or in baking bread. However, there is no doubt that the earliest days of such farming took place back in 8000 B.C. in the Middle East, between the Euphrates and Tigris rivers. With the desire to form settlements, rather than remaining nomadic and gathering crops where they grew wild, our ancestors developed the practice of agriculture and civilization was born.

Even before the rise of civilization, the fruits of fermentation were considered gifts from the gods. Wine was probably a happy accident that occurred after someone left fruit juice uncovered for a day or two and noticed the foamy froth that began to appear on its surface. Then that brave, and lucky, person tasted and enjoyed. It has been suggested that the original beer was discovered when prehistoric man (or woman), having let a bowl of grain mush sit for a day or so, sipped the frothy liquid that rose to the surface.

One of the by-products of civilization is the establishment of a complex system of social order. At the top of this social order were the priests. There is little question as to who got the best of the harvest, as well as the "responsibility" of making sure that wine and beer were made especially to please the gods. Artifacts have been recovered that place beer at the tables of the priests of Ninkasa and Isis.

It was not long before people began to think twice about the idea of reserving beer for only priests or royalty. And it was not long after that happened that beer became an even more egalitarian beverage.

Ancient texts indicate that after a hard day, the Sumerians, who lived at about 3000 B.C., used straws made from reeds to draw off the fermented liquid from special containers of fermented grain and water. This beer played an important part in Sumerian culture and was consumed by men and women from all social classes. Beer parlors received special mention in the Code of Hammurabi in the eighteenth century B.C. Stiff penalties were dealt out to owners who overcharged customers (death by drowning) or who failed to notify authorities of criminals in their establishments (execution). In the Sumerian and Akkadian dictionaries being studied today, the word for *beer* is listed in sections relating to medicine, ritual, and myth.

What might this beer have tasted like? The brewers at the Anchor Brewing Company in San Francisco, California, were looking for a special event to celebrate the tenth anniversary of their new brew house. They saw an article published by bioanthropologist Solomon H. Katz of the University Museum, University of Pennsylvania, that described the beer of the ancient Sumerians. Here was their opportunity to brew, literally, a classic. They took up the challenge and, with the help of historians, produced a beer that, according to a member of the staff of the University Museum, "had the smoothness and effervescence of champagne and a slight aroma of dates." Those Sumerians had been on to something good!

When beer found its way to ancient Egypt, it was once again considered a drink for only the royal. This beer was made of grain, ginger, and honey, sweetened with date sugar. To lengthen the drinkable "life" of the beer, its alcohol content was raised through the addition of more date sugar.

THE EUROPEAN CONNECTION

As civilization spread north, across the Mediterranean, so did beer. The Greeks called the Egyptian beer a "barley wine" and introduced it to the Romans, who passed it to other civilizations as they traveled through Europe.

Of course, wine is a lot easier to make than beer. All you do is harvest the grapes, crush the juice from them, let that juice ferment, and drink it. The climate of the Mediterranean was, and still is, ideal for the growing of grapes. Vines were planted specifically for wine production before Greece had conquered the world.

In Northern Europe, where grain grew in abundance, the preference for beer was drawn by agricultural whim. Where grapes grew in abundance, wine was the beverage of choice. Beer and brewing took hold and flourished where grains were a staple for survival. The Mediterranean area produced wine, and the rich breadbasket of Europe became the cradle for the development of beer.

Evidence of the early history of brewing in Europe is meager, but reveals that brewing was done by the women as part of maintaining a proper household. The entire family drank fermented beverages made from grain. These were nutritious and not nearly as dangerous to drink as the contaminated waters found near most towns and villages. (It must be remembered that what we consider common sanitary practices in the world we live in today were not practiced at that time. Potable water was hard to come by in towns because of less-than-efficient human waste disposal. In rural areas ground water was suspect, and spring water was often not near.)

MONASTIC BEERS .

When the end of the classical Roman and Greek civilizations came, followed by the demise of the Holy Roman Empire, the monasteries of Europe were the sole providers of healers, teachers, preachers, and beer. In those times, transportation was by foot, horse, or cart. Travel, at its best, was tedious and dangerous. In this climate, a tradition of hospitality was practiced by the monasteries that became way stations for pilgrims going from one shrine to another and for travelers seeking refuge on a long journey. All visitors were offered refreshment, a place to rest, and, of course, a chance to offer prayers and donations for their benefactors. The monks and priests were dedicated to various religious and other pursuits, which included humility, poverty, waging wars, the study of nature, illuminating books, and brewing beer as a subsistence beverage. Some religious groups had such strict dietary restrictions that "liquid bread" was the foundation of their existence. Beer, brewed by the members of the religious community, was the beverage offered to the visitors. Some monasteries also provided beer for trade, sale, or barter with their neighbors.

At that time, herbs and spices were the pharmacy of those who knew how to unlock their secrets. The hop plant was used for many things: as a sedative (in pillows), in shampoo (the oils), and as a leather preservative (resins and oils). The first recorded mention of hops in relation to brewing is found in the twelfth-century writings of Hildegarde, the Benedictine nun who was abbess of Rupertsberg, near Mainz, Germany. Her writings specifically suggest that hops retard the spoilage of beer.

This knowledge was important to every monastery and brewing guild that wanted to expand its market. For these producers it was important that the beer they brewed and shipped would last the journey intact and be a credit to their brewing skills. Hops made it possible for beer to endure long trips from the brewery where it was brewed to the consumer who was paying for a product superior to what was available as an everyday beverage. (This may sound familiar to the beer mavens of today!)

With the growth of cities and the greater use of roads, sea lanes, and caravan routes, the market for beer became intercontinental.

KEGS TO GO

In the beginning, beer was brewed for almost immediate consumption by the family or folk of the manor where it was brewed, as well as in the monastic environment. This "home brew" was aged for a short while in casks, but not long enough for the wood to impart any significant flavor. If beer was lagered in casks, pitch-lined casks were used.

Of course, there was no reason to expect a cask of beer to outlast a serving session. The consumption of casks of "cask-conditioned" ale was usually completed, by those who opened the cask, in the time it took them to drink the contents. Once opened, the quality of the beer very much depended on the ability of those present to finish the keg. A beer brewed to almost 12% alcohol by volume and liberally hopped could last for what was in those days a lifetime!

The next "great leap forward" came with the invention of pasteurization. The process prevented spoilage, and it was easier to control the amount of carbonation when it was "forced" into the beer after pasteurization. With a pasteurized beer a brewer needed only to create an extensive distribution network before he was on his way to providing "national" brands. (He also needed a container that made it practical to ship individual servings of a product that was as fresh as it could be.)

BOTTLED BEER

The beginning of bottled beer dates from the discovery of pasteurization. The Franco-Prussian war in 1870 had halted the German beer supply to France. In 1875, Louis Pasteur developed a process of preserving wine and beer from spoiling because of the need to put the French brewing industry on a level with the Germans. Under pressure to keep the home front and the troops happy, he carried out experiments proving that the spoilage of fermented liquids was caused by bacteria. Ergo, yeast free of bacteria produces a fermented beer free of disease.

Pasteur found that by steaming the finished product he could kill all harmful bacteria that cause beer and wine to spoil. This steaming process, soon to become known as "pasteurization," was done by putting filled, well-corked bottles into a water bath that was gradually heated (through the use of steam) to 170°F. This heat was sufficient to kill all yeast and bacteria in the solution. It supposedly had little effect on the flavor of the beverage.

Emil Christian Hansen, a Danish biochemist, was to go one step further than Pasteur and prove that certain yeasts, once identified, were harmful in the fermentation process. He worked to produce an absolutely pure culture which would prove best suited for the manufacturing of beer. In November 1883 he introduced a pure yeast culture at the Carlsburg Brewery. The discoveries of Pasteur and Hansen are of great significance in the development of bottled beer.

. Many of America's breweries made wide use of these scientific breakthroughs to expand their marketing areas. Some of the larger American breweries quickly adopted these discoveries. William J. Uihlein, one of the six brothers who inherited Joseph Schlitz's brewery, brought a pure culture back to America from Copenhagen in 1883. Pabst also adopted the use of pure culture in 1887. Nevertheless, many small breweries in the United States did not take advantage of modern technology. They continued to use "family secret" formulas until the advent of Prohibition. Because of this, many small breweries were not able to produce a high-quality product that could compete with the more scientific larger breweries.

Bottled beer began to gain favor from the time that brewers were able to produce it in pasteurized form. For now the beer could be bottled with the assurance that it would not spoil. Even beer made from impure yeast cultures could be made to last by using the "steaming process."

The glass industry found a friend in Louis Pasteur. Pasteurization required glass companies to produce a strong bottle that could withstand sudden changes in temperature. Once this was accomplished, great demand was made on the glass companies to produce bottles in exceedingly large numbers to satisfy the rapid increase in sales of bottled beer.

Adolphus Busch was the first to take advantage of widespread use of bottled beer. He blanketed the country with "The King of Bottled Beer" by the mid-1870s and opened the eyes of the brewing industry. In a short time, after Busch proved that beer bottling was economically practical, most other larger breweries followed suit.

What makes the story of bottled beer even more interesting is the curious relationship brewers had to bottled beer. At first, most brewers did not do their own bottling, but set up concessions for those who were willing to do the bottling for them.

Those who ran their own bottling departments began to call themselves "brewers and bottlers."

Of course, at the time when bottling shops were being established, the Congress of the United States was busy passing laws saying that the bottling of beer could not take place in the brewery, warehouse, or any place on brewery premises. (The bottling operation had to be done in a building entirely separated from the brewery.) Casks of beer used in the bottling process had to be carried over the surface of a street or road that was commonly used by the public. This was decreed so that all the beer produced had to be put in casks or kegs for taxing purposes. All bottled beer had to come from kegs on which the government had already collected taxes.

On June 18, 1890, through the efforts of Fred Pabst, the Internal Revenue Act was changed to allow "the construction of pipelines from storage cellars to bottling houses." The bottling house and the brewery still had to remain separate, but the pipeline made bottling much more efficient. The beer was run through a gauge, and a tax collector was on hand to see that the appropriate amount of revenue was collected. This method remained in effect up until the time of Prohibition.

After Prohibition, the business of "economy of volume" took over. Metal kegs of pressurized beer were the harbingers of doom to the small brewer. Large companies could afford the metal (easily returnable/reusable) kegs, which could be filled with enough beer to keep a bartender busy for a few days. All that was needed was some additional ingredients to keep the beer looking and tasting "fresh" after a long, rough journey from brewer to consumer.

As you will see in Chapter 5, "Beers of the United States," Prohibition and the ensuing two decades of "big is better" almost killed the brewing industry in this country. It was the lead of the California vintners that restarted the art of brewing in the United States.

CHAPTER FOUR

Styles of Beer

BEER FROM TOP TO BOTTOM

In order to fully understand the concept of beer "syles," we must pay a visit to our friends in the world of wine.

For someone just learning about wine, the customary starting-off point is "red" and "white." The next step is usually to explore a geographic area where the wines with which the imbiber wants to become familiar are produced. This makes understanding the production, the names of the viticulture areas, and the names of the wineries easier to understand. Starting out with an elaborate explanation of the pecking order of Bordeaux vineyards to a neophyte serves only to confuse and discourage. The same can be said for presenting those of you just developing an appreciation of beer with a technical organizational chart of the maze of styles developed by those who have an almost religious devotion to beer and brewing.

WHAT IS A STYLE?

All of the beers brewed before the mid-1800s were essentially what we now call "ales." The only exceptions were the "lagers" of southern Germany. Bavarian brewers knew that if they stored their beers in ice-cold caves in the piedmont of the Alps during the spring and summer months, the resulting beers were smoother and drier than beers that were not "lagered." Over time this resulted in the selective survival of the only yeasts that could survive this cold storage—bottom-fermenting (lager) yeast. It was not until 1841 (30 years before Pasteur's work) that the Munich brewer Gabriel Sedlmeyer isolated a strain of bottom-fermenting yeast and began the brewing and fermenting of what we now know as lager beer. Briefly, let's review the characteristics of the two yeasts that are used to ferment both ale and lager beers.

ALE YEAST

Top-fermenting ale yeast is a quick-working yeast that thrives at temperatures between 60 and 70°F and produces by-products of fermentation called esters, which add the "flowery" aromas of apple, pear, pineapple, grass, hay, plum, and prune that are characteristic of ale.

LAGER YEAST

Lager, a German word meaning "to store," is the perfect word to define a brew that is kept for more than 30 days in a cold, dark place. This is necessary because the yeast used to ferment a lager beer works slowly, and at temperatures close to 34°F. Lager yeast produces fewer aromatics than ale yeast. The resulting lack of esters allows the aroma of the hops used in the brew to remain in the forefront, complementing the sweet flavor of the malt.

STYLES OF BEER AND HOW THEY CAME TO BE

To put the idea of different styles in context, it must be remembered that before the Industrial Revolution most beer was brewed to meet the demands of a family, town, or neighborhood. Beer was consumed because the water, even in rural areas, was not considered potable. The ingredients used to make this beer were from materials close at hand. The local water played a major role in this process. Hard water made the best ales, and soft water made the best lagers. Local hops were used, when economical, to add unique flavors. Each strain of hop, having its own flavor, lent a special character to a local beer. Other ingredients were used to make the basic sweet, alcoholic beer meet the tastes and cuisine of a particular locality.

It is also important to note that, as today, the cost of the ingredients determined the cost of the finished product. Everyday beer was made from as little malt (sugar) as possible and was therefore low in alcohol content and relatively inexpensive. A good example of this style was called "small beer," which was consumed by the masses in the United Kingdom as a staple beverage.

Local tradition, as well as economy, determined the ratio of roasted malts and various hop varieties that would determine the style of a local beverage and its specific flavor characteristics. In some cases the use of wild yeast created special beers called "lambics."

HOW MANY STYLES OF BEER ARE THERE?

Although there are only two types of beer (ale and lager), both of these include a number of styles. Basically, there are approximately 16 styles of beer and ale. The determination of what constitutes a style has been generally codified by brewers and organizations such as the Master Brewers Association of America, Association of Brewers, American Homebrewers Association, CAMRA, and other professional organizations (not to mention beer writers who never miss an opportunity to argue over what makes a style legitimate). The following pages describe these styles, listing them generally from the lightest, most delicate flavored, to the dark, strong-flavored specialty brews.

The essential difference is the content of the brew. As each chateau has a "signature" that wine connoisseurs can readily detect, certain geographic areas also provide signature brews that are just as distinct. The basis for a particular style is usually found in the basic ingredients of the brew that are indigenous to a specific area. Another influence is the local cuisine. (As you will see in Chapter 11, "Beer and Food," cuisine and beer are much more compatible than you would first imagine.)

The beers I have chosen are the essential examples, those I consider to be the epitome of the individual styles. I use specific brands so that you will have a benchmark when tasting similar beers of a particular style.

It is important that you know the "real thing" when you taste it. It should be similar to the sensual experience of first tasting genuine Roquefort Bleu cheese or a ripe tomato, fresh off the vine. The Roquefort put all other blue cheeses in context, and that just-picked tomato gave you a different perspective on all those gas-ripened, hothouse, supermarket tomatoes you once paid way too much for.

The Style Sheet

The following pages do not list every style of beer known to brewers. I chose these styles because they offer a sufficiently broad range of taste experiences to introduce you to the "essential" styles of beer. I do hope you become intrigued enough to search for even more esoteric styles. I can guarantee it will prove to be quite an adventure.

1. AMERICAN LIGHT LAGER

This style of beer is the result of the growth of national breweries and their ability to produce a beer with the widest possible appeal at a competitive price. It is essentially a pilsner-style lager, brewed with significant quantities of grain other than barley malt. It is a slightly sweet, lightly hopped, straw-colored, very effervescent beer.

BUDWEISER

Anheuser-Busch uses nine different hops and special yeast to impart an apple-like flavor and aroma to what is really a rather complex beer. Information from the brewer also notes that the grist for Budweiser consists of both two-row and six-row malted bar-

BUDWEISER, AN AMERICAN LIGHT LAGER

ley. (According to the same source, rice is added to impart a dry "snap" to the flavor.)

Beech wood is used in the fermentation process to aid in increasing the area for the yeast to be exposed to the wort. A layer of beech wood chips, cleaned and rinsed before use, is spread on the bottom of the lager tanks to provide more surface area for the action of the yeast.

A 12-ounce serving of Budweiser contains approximately 142 calories, 11.1 grams of carbohydrates, and 1.2 grams of protein. It is cholesterol-free and falls in the FDA's "Very Low" sodium category.

Alcohol content: 4.8% by volume.

2. EUROPEAN PILSNER

This style is a light-straw-colored, full bodied, lagered, bottom-fermented beer named after the town of Plzeň (in what was then known as Bohemia), where it was first brewed in 1842. It quickly became a popular unique style because it was so different from the amber brews that were the norm at that time.

PILSNER URQUELL

Pilsner Urquell (literally "original from Plzeň"), named for the town of Plzeň, in what is now the Czech Republic, was the first golden-colored lager developed in the nineteenth century. Until that time, almost all brews—ale and lager—were amber colored or darker.

Pilsner Urquell is, for the most part, still brewed as it was in the late 1800s, when the brewery was refitted with modern nineteenth-century technology. Today Pilsner Urquell is brewed with water from the same artesian wells that provided water for the original brewers. The brew has a white head with average size and density; it features a golden color and a nice malty aroma with subtle spicy undertones. The grist is Czech malt, and the hops are 100% Saaz, from the Zatec region.

Alcohol content: 4.4% alcohol by volume.

Pilsner Urquell, a European Pilsner

3. British Bitter

This top-fermented classic-ale style offers a deep, rich brown or ruby color with a malty, very lightly hopped flavor. True bitter is only lightly carbonated.

FULLER'S LONDON PRIDE

Fuller's London Pride is the flagship brew of the Fuller's brewery in London. It offers the soft texture, full malt flavor, and honey-flower character of the house yeast. Not a dry-hopped ale, this is a great example of a traditional British "session" beer—one that is meant to be enjoyed, pint after pint, with good friends in a friendly pub. Recently made available in the United States on draft, it also is shipped in bottles.

Alcohol content: 4.1% by volume.

4. PALE ALE

Pale ale, another classic British top-fermented ale style, has more hop flavor than bitter, but not as much as India pale ale. (There is a good measure of overlap when other than mainstream examples of British bitter, pale ale, and India pale ale are compared.)

BASS

Bass Ale has been brewed in Burton-on-Trent since 1777. The hard water there, perfect for brewing pale ales, is combined with local barley and hops to create a deep amber-colored brew that was first labeled as pale ale. Bass now carries the appellation "IPA," for India pale ale (although it is no longer brewed specifically to that style). Bass Ale is a classic British pale ale with good amber color, a malty flavor, and Kent hops for bittering and aroma.

The bottled and kegged products are identical except for different carbonation levels. (The bottle has more sparkle.)

Alcohol content: 5% by volume.

Bass Pale Ale

5. India Pale Ale

India pale ale, so named because it had to endure long sea voyages from breweries in England to outposts on the fringes of the British Empire, had to be a high-gravity, well-hopped brew to enable it to last the voyage and not spoil. Although there are some fine examples still brewed in the United Kingdom, Liberty Ale (brewed in the United States by Anchor Brewing Company, San Francisco, California) is a particularly well-balanced brew.

 ### LIBERTY ALE

Liberty Ale was released in 1975 as Anchor's original Christmas beer. It is a top-fermented ale, naturally carbonated, and dry-hopped for a very floral aroma and dry flavor.

Alcohol content: Not released.

6. Vienna Lager

This style was once the style "à la mode" in Vienna at the turn of the nineteenth century. Then it fell from fashion and left Europe for the warmer climate of Mexico. Today, the only true "Vienna" lager is Dos Equis, but with the growth of the specialty beer market it may not hold its special place for long.

DOS EQUIS

The unique, almost red, color and roasted malt flavor of Dos Equis is the result of the judicious use of special crystal malt (a malt that is roasted before it has dried after sprouting and gives a unique color and flavor to the beer) and roasted malt. Traditional hops and special water treatments result in a beer from Mexico that is a good example of the color and flavor of what was once a popular style of the beer brewed, almost exclusively, in Vienna, Austria.

Alcohol content: 4.7% by volume.

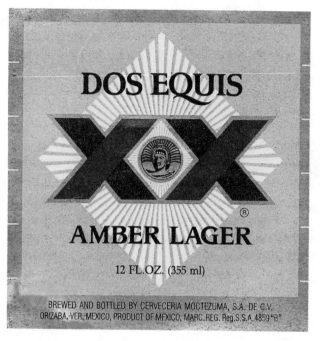

Dos Equis, a Vienna Lager

7. Brown Ale

Brown Ale is a traditional British ale. Top fermented, it is similar to a pale ale but sweeter and darker.

NEWCASTLE BROWN ALE

Newcastle Brown Ale was created in Newcastle-upon-Tyne in the northeast of England during the 1920s. Distinct in color, it has a nutlike flavor and a fine head. It is sold in the United States in 12-ounce bottles, British "pint" bottles, and on draft.

Alcohol content: 4.7% by volume.

Newcastle Brown Ale

8. Scottish Ale

This is a strong (high alcohol) brew made with Scottish malted barley. Less hoppy than English brews, there are hints of caramel and, sometimes, a slight tang of smoke in the flavor (from peat fuel used to roast the malt).

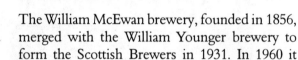

MCEWAN'S SCOTCH ALE

The William McEwan brewery, founded in 1856, merged with the William Younger brewery to form the Scottish Brewers in 1931. In 1960 it underwent another incarnation and become part of Scottish & Newcastle. Today, the McEwan's Scotch Ale is still brewed at McEwan's Fountain Brewery in Edinburgh, Scotland.

McEwan's Scotch Ale is strong, rich, and very dark brown in appearance, not quite opaque. The aroma is a combination of malt and alcohol, with a slight roast tinge. In the mouth, the beer is full-bodied, smooth, and malty sweet. In the finish, the sweetness is offset by a hint of roastiness.

Alcohol content: 5.1% by volume.

McEwan's Scotch Ale

9. Strong Ale

Also called "Old Ale," this strong (high alcohol) brew is particular for its dark color and a very sweet malt flavor that masks the heat of an alcohol content that can reach 6–8% by volume.

THEAKSTON'S OLD PECULIER

No, the brewmaster was not tippling when he spelled the name of this beer. *Webster's Unabridged* defines a *peculier* as "a church or parish exempt from the jurisdiction of the ordinary in whose territory it lies" (an ordinary, of course, being "a prelate exercising actual ecclesiastical jurisdiction over a specified territory"). Graced with the seal of the official of the peculier of Masham on its label, the name "Old Peculier" finally makes sense.

This rather special brew, made from pale ale and crystal malts, wheat, caramel, and three types of sugar, is a very high-gravity beer. Fuggles is the most prevalent hop used, but it is used in concert with Northern Brewer for balance. The yeast is a mixed strain, rather than pure culture. This has helped it endure for more than 30 years.

Theakston's Old Peculier is imported into the United States by Scottish & Newcastle. The product is sold only in bottles in the United States. Those lucky enough to travel to Yorkshire and sample this beer from the cask will truly have an experience they will want to tell their grandchildren about.

Alcohol content: 6–8% by volume.

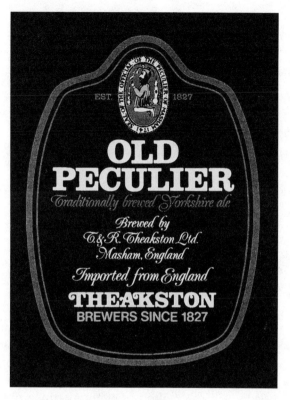

Theakston's Old Peculier, a Strong Ale

10. BARLEYWINE

Barleywine is a very dark, almost opaque ale. The term "barleywine" is fairly new. Once classified as a strong ale, it has now become a separate style. This is the most alcoholic style of beer. The addition of a healthy amount of hops forms a powerful flavor triad of sweet malt, bitter hops, and warm alcohol. Alcohol content can reach 10% by volume

ANCHOR OLD FOGHORN

First brewed in 1975, Old Foghorn Barleywine Style Ale became available year-round in 1985.

Brewed in small batches, to maintain an extremely high original gravity, Old Foghorn is top-fermented and dry-hopped. Although there are other "barleywines" brewed in the United States and the United Kingdom, this particular beer is packed to the gunwales with hops, yet manages to balance a body of almost epic proportions and high alcohol content fit for a seadog.

Alcohol content: Not released.

Old Foghorn Barleywine Style Ale

11. Bock Beer

*This style is similar to strong ale but it is fermented with
bottom-fermenting yeast and is lagered (aged) for at least one month.
This is truly a substantial beer, as is noted in the following profile.*

SALVATOR

Italian monks of the order of St. Francis, invited
to Munich in 1624 during the Counter-Reformation period, led a very strict existence. Their religious beliefs forbade the consumption of meat, butter, milk, and eggs, and allowed only fish, bread, vegetables, and vegetarian liquids. In order to supplement their poor nutrition, the Paulaner monks learned to brew a special beer. In 1627 a Father Barnabas began brewing a dark beer, rich in nutrients necessary for the continued survival of his order.

When the monks got permission from the local court to sell their beer to the local population in 1780, they produced a doppel bock (a beer similar to a barleywine except that it is fermented with a bottom-fermenting yeast), which they called Salvator (pronounced sal-vah-tor). This was the mother of double bocks. Other double bocks put "-ator" at the ends of their names in honor of this fine brew.

The tradition is commemorated with the depiction, on the label, of Father Barnabas presenting a mug of Salvator to the Duke of Bavaria.

Alcohol content: 7.5% by volume.

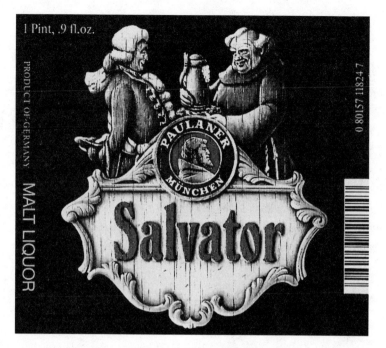

Salvator, a Bock Beer

12. PORTER

*Originally, porter was a dark, top-fermented beer, economically
produced for everyday consumption by the working class of the U.K.
It is a sad fact that the "porter" of Charles Dickens's time is gone.
The day when porter "died" there were funeral processions held in the
United Kingdom to mark the event. There are some alive who
remember the day. Although the specific yeast is not used any more,
the style lives on in the United States, where there are brewers who
will not give up the ghost. Although there are a number of
micro-breweries now producing porter-style beers, they must, through
default, compare themselves with "The Celebrated Pottsville Porter."*

YEUNGLING'S PORTER

For those in the know, this is a real "sleeper."
Brewed in Pottsville, Pennsylvania, by the Yeungling Brewery since 1914, this is a dry, roasty brew
that is darker than amber and lighter than stout. Yeungling has
the malt for its porter specially roasted to give it a unique flavor.

Alcohol content: 5% by volume.

13. Stout

This is a top-fermented, opaque, dark, rich brew that could be called the national beer of Ireland.

GUINNESS STOUT

Although there are many stouts brewed both in the United States and in the Republic of Ireland, Guinness Stout is perceived as the touchstone for all stouts. To ensure quality control, Guinness roasts malt specifically for its own production needs. All the grain used by Guinness is grown in Ireland. The assortment of roasted malts is complemented by the addition of 25% flaked barley and 10% roasted barley.

The hops are mostly Kent Goldings, and fermentation is done with a strain of the brew's original yeast, isolated in the early 1960s. The yeast works at high temperatures (about 25°C/77°F).

Alcohol content: (bottles) 5.6% alcohol by volume.
(draft, can) 4.2% alcohol by volume.

GUINNESS STOUT

14. Wheat Beer

Wheat beer, with usually 30% malted wheat added to the grist, is especially popular in Bavaria. It is also a popular style with Belgian brewers.

 ## *PAULANER HEFE-WEIZEN*

Paulaner Hefe-Weizen starts with a two-mash process using dark- and light-colored brewing malt from two-row Bavarian summer barley, dark- and light-colored malted wheat, and caramelized malt. This top-fermented beer contains more than half wheat. Hallertau hops are used for both bittering and aroma. Lager yeast is used for bottling, and the beer is allowed to lager for approximately two to three weeks at −1°C.

Alcohol content: 5.5% by volume.

Paulaner Hefe-Weizen, a Wheat Beer

15. Belgian Styles

A full explanation of the Belgian styles can be found in "Beers of Belgium" in Chapter 7.

Flanders Red Ales

RODENBACH

Among the "red beers," Rodenbach is considered the quintessential example of the style. Visitors to the brewery in Roeselaere can see the 300 oak casks (the brewery has four coopers to maintain the tuns), all more than 20 feet high, where the beer is aged. Rodenbach is brewed from four malts, one pale from summer barley, two-

Rodenbach, a Belgian Style Flanders Red Ale

and six-row varieties of winter malted barley, and crystal (Vienna) roasted malt. The hops are mainly Brewer's Gold, with some Kent Goldings. Five different strains of yeast are used in the fermentation process.

Alcohol content: 4.6% by volume.

Lambic

LINDEMANS KRIEK

Lindemans Kriek is a top-fermented cherry-flavored lambic (70% malted barley and 30% unmalted wheat) with a rose color. It has an aroma of cherries and is very sparkling, refreshing with a dry finish. The acidic flavor of the lambic blends well with the cherry

Lindemans Kriek Lambic

flavor. This beer is best served in a champagne flute at 45°F. It is sold in 750 ml bottles.

Alcohol content: Not released.

Lambic

LINDEMANS GUEUZE

Gueuze, possibly the oldest beer style still in general production, is unseasoned wheat beer, fermented with the ambient yeast from the region in and around Brussels. It is prized by beer lovers who "lay it down" in a cool, dark place, like fine wine.

Lindemans Gueuze is golden-colored, with a cidery, winelike flavor. It is similar in flavor profile to a sparkling vermouth.

Alcohol content: 6.1% by volume.

LINDEMANS GUEUZE LAMBIC

Lambic

LIEFMANS FRAMBOZENBIER

Most Belgian frambozenbier is made from lambic beers infused with fruit. Liefmans Frambozenbier is made from a base of Goudenband Brown Ale. This beer was introduced in Belgium in October, 1985.

The main flavor is the winelike taste of the brown ale. The raspberry flavor quickly becomes evident, and the finish is sharp and refreshing. This is a very effervescent beverage, even more lively than the weiss beers of Munich.

Liefmans Frambozenbier

This beer should be stored, and served, just slightly chilled to fully appreciate the aroma of the raspberries and the flavor of the ale.

Alcohol content: 5.0% by volume.

BELGIAN STRONG

DUVEL

Duvel is brewed by the Moorgat brewery in Breendonk, Belgium. It is regarded as the quintessential pale strong ale, with a flavor that is complex and deep. It is made with Danish summer barley malt, whole-flower Styrian and Saaz hops. Duvel undergoes three fermentations. The first is warm, the second cold, and the final one takes place in the bottle, lasting five weeks, before being shipped.

Alcohol content: 8.5% by volume.

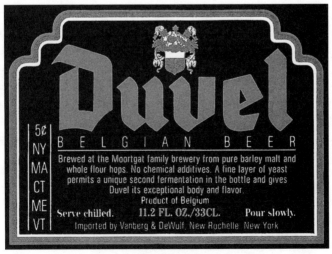

DUVEL, A BELGIAN STRONG BEER

Trappist

CHIMAY

Chimay (pronounced "she-MAY") produces three types of Trappist beers, identified by the color of the metal cap that tops their distinctive cork-finished bottles: Premier Chimay (red), Cinq Cents (white), and Grand Reserve (blue).

The red, as well as the blue, has a very particular "house character" that is fruity and sweetish, with a soft, full, deep body. This beer is dark brown with a ruby hue. The white Chimay is much hoppier and drier, with a quenching hint of acidity. It also has a paler color, more amber than ruby red.

Alcohol content:

>Premier Chimay (red), 7% by volume.
>Cinq Cents (white), 8% by volume.
>Grand Reserve (blue), 9% by volume.

16. Specialty Beers

These unique beers do not fit easily into any particular style. Each is considered to stand alone as a special beer.

Steam Beer

Today, "Steam Beer" is a trademark of the Anchor Brewing Company of San Francisco, California. In the nineteenth century, steam beer was a nickname for local beers that were fermented with lager yeast at ale-yeast temperature, producing beers with ale-like character. It may also have been common practice to top off kegs of beer with beer that had not finished its first fermentation. The result was an in-keg fermentation that produced high levels of natural carbonation. With no refrigeration to control this fermentation, a freshly tapped keg would produce copious amounts of foam or "steam."

 ### *ANCHOR STEAM BEER*

Anchor Steam Beer is the standard of a style of hoppy, malty beer. It has the crisp flavor features of a lager, and the esters (fruitiness), complex aromas, and flavor base of an ale. Dark amber in color, the grist is American-grown malt (pale and roasted) and hops are from the American Northwest.

Alcohol content: Not released.

Herbed/Spiced

ANCHOR OUR SPECIAL ALE

Every year since 1975, Anchor has brewed a Christmas Ale. It is produced in small quantities and is available only from late November until early January. Each year the recipe is changed, and there is a special label designed around the tree, a traditional symbol of renewal. Properly refrigerated, this beer remains drinkable for years.

Alcohol content: Not released.

ANCHOR OUR SPECIAL ALE, 1994

Smoked

KAISERDOM RAUCHBIER

Kaiserdom is brewed in Bamberg, Germany, from malt that has been smoked in a way similar to the process of smoking malted barley in the making of Scotch whiskey. The technique of smoking malted barley to dry it and add color was used before the more modern method of indirect kilning was introduced.

Kaiserdom Rauchbier is brewed from Bavarian barley that has been roasted over a fire of moist beech wood logs. Whole Hallertau hops are used to provide flavor and aroma. The fermentation is a bottom fermentation, and the beer is lagered

Kaiserdom Rauchbier, a Smoked Beer

for three months. The finished product is a beer of conventional alcohol content, with a dark color and complex smoky flavor characteristics.

Alcohol content: 4.21% by weight.

STRONG LAGER

SAMICHLAUS BIER

Brewed just one day a year, on December 6 (St. Nicholas Day) in Switzerland, Samichlaus is aged for 10 months before bottling for the American market. The beer is bottled for a full year in Switzerland. Samichlaus is brewed with two-row summer barley malt (Pilsner and Munich styles), two varieties of Hallertau hops,

Bottled in 1994

Samichlaus

RARE IMPORTED SWISS BEER.

Bier®

Brewed only once a year on December 6, Samichlaus Bier is patiently aged for a full eleven months before bottling.

355ml 12 fl. oz.

Brewed and bottled in Switzerland by Brauerei Hurlimann AG, Zurich

Imported by Phoenix Imports, Ltd., Baltimore, MD

SAMICHLAUS BIER, A STRONG LAGER

and special yeast that can metabolize in a high-alcohol environment. Samichlaus begins with 3 pounds of dissolved solids in each gallon of wort (weighing 10 pounds), and after fermentation there is still ¼ pound of unfermented solids in each gallon of finished beer. Although it is a lager, this beer should be stored and served at cellar temperature (50°F) in order to fully appreciate its flavor and aroma.

Samichlaus has been called "the world's strongest lager" by many beer experts, but has recently been eclipsed by Samuel Adams "Triple Bock" at close to 17% by volume.

Alcohol content: 14.9% by volume.

Oktoberfest

PAULANER OKTOBERFEST MARZEN

Traditionally, when the last of the winter season's beer was brewed each year in March, it was made to be a little stronger than usual so that the alcohol content would preserve it through the summer. By then the beer was very well attenuated and sporting a relatively high alcohol content. Today that tradition continues with the brewing of Marzen, or "March Beer."

Paulaner Marzen starts with a two-mash process using dark- and light-colored brewing malt from two-row Bavarian summer barley. Hallertau hops are used for both bittering and aroma. Lager yeast is used, and the beer is allowed to lager for approximately four weeks at –1°C.

Alcohol content: 5% by volume.

CHAPTER
FIVE

Beers of the United States

COLONIAL BREWING

The arrival of the Pilgrims at Plymouth Rock in 1620 marked the first major colonization of what would become the United States. Their original destination was "Hudson's River," but because of less-than-perfect navigation and other problems while crossing a less-than-friendly Atlantic Ocean, they found themselves off the coast of Cape Cod. The captain and crew of the *Mayflower* insisted that they disembark there, because if more time was spent looking for another site, there would not be enough beer for the crew to survive the trip back to England. The Pilgrims had no choice but to settle where they landed.

As the nineteenth century approached, three distinct developments were evident in the brewing industry. Philadelphia and New York increased their prominence, while brewing in New England declined appreciably. At the same time new centers and markets for brewers were emerging in other parts of the country with the expansion of the frontier.

The beers brewed in Philadelphia drew the praise of the British consul there in 1789, and he reported home that although the porter brewed in that city was not as good as the porter from Bristol, the reason was that its users drank it too soon.

When lager beer reached the market in the United States in the nineteenth century, it was regarded for some time as little more than a novelty. With the development of industrial refrigeration and the immigration of Central Europeans, Germans and Czechs, the thirst for lager beer soon eclipsed the demand for traditional ale. The novelty was fast becoming the norm.

In the second decade of the twentieth century there were more fine dining restaurants in New York City than there were in Paris. The wine cellars of these restaurants, and of many wealthy citizens, rivaled the best of Europe. Chefs were coming to the United States from Europe to experience the wealth of produce that was available. The country was on its way to attaining a true culinary heritage. Then disaster struck!

PROHIBITION

The Volstead Act, the Eighteenth Amendment to the Constitution of the United States of America, was an attempt to legislate social mores espoused by a vocal minority. (It took more than a year to ratify this piece of legislation.) It did not work as expected. In effect, the only lasting result of the Eighteenth Amendment was to entrench organized crime in the United States. Fine restaurants folded and were replaced by hole-in-the-wall "speakeasy" bars.

The Eighteenth Amendment was erased by the Twenty-First Amendment: the only amendment to the United States Constitution enacted to repeal another amendment of that Constitution. (It took only nine months to get this amendment passed.) On December 3, 1933, U.S. citizens took their first legal drink in 14 years. Of the 1,568 breweries in operation in

1910 (brewing more than 63 million barrels a year), only 750 reopened when Prohibition was ended in 1933. Production in that year was just over 2 million barrels. The brewing industry recovered gradually, reaching production of just over 55 million barrels when World War II broke out.

CANNED BEER AND TELEVISION

After the Second World War, you could have your beer three ways: on draft, in bottles, and in cans. (Canned beer was perfected, on a grand scale, to provide beer to the armed forces of the United States during that conflict.) You could have your news three ways too: newspapers, radio, and television (actually, four: there were still barber shops). All of this affected the brewing and appreciation of beer in the United States.

The following years were a time of prosperity for most North Americans. There was an optimistic belief that there was no limit to expansion of science, technology, democracy, or economy. The economy of size was a golden idol. Larger size meant lower overhead cost per item and ease of production. It was a time of canned beer and white bread. Gradually, the local breweries that survived Prohibition had to close because they couldn't compete with cans of beer sold for half of what it cost them to sell a bottle of their beer. Then the regional brewers folded under the onslaught of the nationwide advertising that created a demand for national products. It almost came down to only a few brewing companies in the entire United States: Anheuser-Busch, Miller, Schlitz, Pabst, and Ballantine were the top contenders.

In 1957, Anheuser-Busch knocked Schlitz out of first place in the U.S. brewing industry. In 1970, Miller held seventh place in the industry, but tobacco giant Philip Morris acquired Miller and began a long, fierce challenge to Budweiser's leadership. By 1978, Miller passed Schlitz and Pabst to take second place, but Anheuser-Busch triumphed, becoming the first brewer to sell 40 million barrels a year. Soon the two top brewers were producing more than 50 percent of the beer sold in America, largely at the expense of smaller, independent breweries.

THE BIRTH OF THE "MICROS"

While the big boys were fighting it out with advertising campaigns and discounting practices that left them with paper-thin profit margins, something was happening in California. There had never been any doubt that the vineyards of California could produce very servicable *vin ordinare*, but it had been financially impractical to strive for greater glory until, through the use of a section of the tax laws known as "Limited Partnership," the rich soil of the Napa, Sonoma, and Mendicino valleys gave birth to a number of "boutique wineries." These wineries would soon prove that the United States could produce world-class wines with personality.

This example was followed closely by a new breed of brewers. These were people who had tasted the fine beers of Europe and wondered why similar beers could not be brewed in the United States. They began brewing beer at home, and introducing friends and neighbors to the pleasures of their rich, full-bodied brews.

In the same creative atmosphere that gave birth to the multitude of boutique wineries, the "micro brewery" was born.

Until the early 1970s, U.S. breweries, for the most part, brewed a pale imitation of a pilsner style of beer. Then, in 1974, in New Albion, California, the McAuslands began brewing "amber" ale. That was just the beginning. The next 20 years would see the number of breweries in the United States grow from a handful to more than 400 by 1994.

THE U.S. BREWING SCENE TODAY

Today there is no country on earth with as many styles of beer being brewed as there are now being brewed and consumed in the United States. The brewers of mass-produced, premium-priced beer have watched the growth of specialty beers and imports. Although specialty beers now make up only 2% of the beer market, all four of the top brewers have ventured into this segment.

Coors has cemented ties to Australia with a licensing agreement to produce Castlemaine XXXX in the United States; Miller controls a portion of Molson; and Molson produces Foster's Lager (Australia) in Canada.

THE TOP THREE

The following pages give a brief profile of the top three major brewers: Anheuser-Busch, Miller Brewing Company, and Coors Brewing Company. These three companies produce almost 80% of all the beer brewed in the United States.

ANHEUSER-BUSCH

**One Busch Place
St. Louis, MO 63188
314-577-2000**

In 1852, George Schneider founded what was called the Bavarian Brewery in St. Louis, Missouri. Eight years later he sold the brewery to Eberhard Anheuser. Anheuser's son-in-law, Adolphus Busch, who joined the company in 1865, was inspired by the lager beers of Germany. In 1876, with restaurateur Carl Conrad, he created a light-colored lager beer he called Budweiser, after the town of Budweis, in Bavaria. By 1901, Budweiser was selling at a rate of one million barrels annually.

When Adolphus died in 1913, his son, August, took over the company. He renamed it Anheuser-Busch, Inc. in 1919, just in time for Prohibition. During those years (1920–1933) the company survived by selling yeast, refrigeration units, truck bodies, malt syrup, and soft drinks. As soon as Prohibition was repealed, Busch was brewing. He personally delivered a case of Budweiser to President Franklin Roosevelt in a carriage drawn by Clydesdale horses, which have since become the symbol of the company.

In 1993 the beer maker bought 18% of Modelo, Mexico's top brewer. The agreement came with an option for Anheuser-Busch to acquire a total of 35% of Modelo, which produces Corona, the number one beer in Mexico.

In 1994 a new beer, Ice Draft, was introduced with success. Also in that year, Japan's Kirin Brewery announced that it would begin buying beer cans and beer (brewed in California but sold in Japan under the Kirin banner) from Anheuser-Busch. A-B has recently signed a distribution agreement with The Red Hook Brewery of Seattle, Washington, acquiring a 15% equity position in Red Hook. It is also producing an ale for the specialty market, called Elk Mountain Ale, brewed with British ale yeast and, through licensing arrangements, is now brewing Budweiser in the United Kingdom.

MILLER BREWING COMPANY

**3939 West Highland Boulevard
Milwaukee, WI 53201
414-931-2000**

In 1850, Charles Best founded the Plank Road Brewery in Milwaukee, Wisconsin. He was soon joined by his brother, and together they formed Best Brothers. The two founded the Menomonee Valley Brewery. Legend has it that this brewery, situated on the road to Wauwatosa, sold its beer to wholesalers in New York City by 1852. Three years later the brewery was bought by Frederick Miller.

Miller made major changes in production and plant design. The company began its own malting in 1865. Artificial refrigeration was introduced in 1886. In 1888 the brewery complex was entirely

Miller High Life Beer

rebuilt. This was also the year that the Frederick Miller Brewing Company went public.

In 1970, Philip Morris purchased Miller Brewing Company and, with aggressive marketing, took it from seventh place to be the second largest brewing company in the United States in just 10 years.

In 1993 the company acquired a 20% interest in Molson, Canada's largest brewer, and 100% of Molson Breweries USA for $320 million.

THE CHARGE OF THE LITE BRIGADE

In 1972 Miller bought rights to the Meister Brau line of products, including one called Lite Beer. Although Lite Beer cost less to produce than regular beers, the Miller Brewing Company positioned it as a premium beer.

The formula for Lite Beer continued to prove a winner, especially because of widespread, aggressive marketing. Miller's goal was to

Miller Lite Beer

convince the public that the low-calorie beer was as suited for men as it was for women. Not only did Miller achieve this goal, it broke ground in the brewing industry by developing the low-calorie/low-carbohydrate beer and made it a national best seller. Here is the story of how that was done.

In 1973, Miller's advertising agency, McCann-Erickson, was given the Lite Beer account. Bob Lenz was the creative group head in charge of the account. He did the usual brand research and found that, for some reason, the beer drinkers of Anderson, Indiana, were head-over-heels in love with this "Lite" beer. This friendly town in the heartland of America had taken Lite to its heart. Men, women, lawyers, carpenters, cops, and truck drivers—anyone who drank beer in Anderson—drank Lite beer. All Lenz had to do was figure out how to convince the rest of America to love low-calorie beer too.

The first piece of the puzzle fell into place while Lenz was riding a bus in New York City. He glanced up at an advertisement for the fledgeling New York Off-Track Betting business. The smiling countenance of ex-New York Jet Matt Snell smiled back at him. Lenz had worked with Snell before, so with a little persuasion, was able to sign him up as the new Lite spokesman. That first television ad was a classic—you probably remember it! There is lovable Matt Snell, sitting in a comfortable-looking barroom (actually Joe Allen's in New York City) with the graphic "Matt Snell Super Bowl Hero" plastered at the bottom of the screen. There is a huge pile of Lite beer cans on the table. Snell begins: "You know, new Lite Beer from Miller is all you ever wanted in a beer . . . and less." Snell then holds up a bottle of Lite and tells you that it is not only low in calories, it is also low in carbohydrates! (a big topic at that time). Finally, as the camera pans back to reveal the pile of beer cans, Snell offers the following (as the FCC requires); "Oh, I'm not saying I drank all this beer myself. I had some help from my friends!" Then comes the punch line: "At six-foot-three, two-thirty, there's a lot of me to fill." That was the start of an advertising campaign that turned Miller Lite into a national institution—and started the "light beer" revolution.

COORS BREWING COMPANY

12th and Ford
Golden, CO 80401
303-279-6565

Adolph Coors was born in 1847 in Barmen, Prussia (today the German city of Wuppertal). When he was 15 years old, young Coors signed on as an apprentice at the Henry Wenker Brewery in Dortmund, Germany. By the time he was 18 years old he had paid off his apprenticeship and gone on to become a paid employee of the brewery.

In 1868, with the winds of change blowing through European politics, young Coors set out for the United States. By late 1869, Coors was employed as a foreman at the Stenger Brewery in Naperville, Illinois. Shortly after that, Adolph Coors found his way to Denver, Colorado, and into the ownership of a bottling company, but he wanted a brewery.

THE GOLDEN BREWERY

When a partnership with a businessman named Jacob Schueler made investment possible, Coors and his partner set up a brewery in Golden, Colorado, and the original Coors beer was introduced in April 1874.

Through Prohibition, the company continued operation by diversifying into similar businesses such as making legal alcohol (for medical and other legal purposes), cement manufacturing, porcelain manufacturing, soft drinks, and candy.

THE COORS CRAZE

In the late 1960s Coors "Banquet" (now Original Coors) was discovered by beer afficionados who were intrigued by the fact that the beer was filtered, not pasteurized.

The one problem with filtered beer is that, unrefrigerated, it can easily spoil. Then, as today, Coors would not ship its beer to a wholesaler or client who could not ensure refrigeration of the product at all times. With a limited distribution area and special care, the Coors beer that was on the market was usually very fresh. Until a national distribution system was in place in the late 1970s, Coors was not widely available. Even then it retained its mystique.

Original Coors is brewed with a strain of barley developed by the Coors Brewing Company, grown for Coors by farmers in Colorado, Wyoming, Idaho, and Montana. It takes about 60 days to brew, lager, package, and distribute this product.

Product data: Original Coors Nutrition: 137 calories/12 ounces

Alcohol content: approximately 4.6 percent alcohol by volume.

ORIGINAL COORS

PRODUCT LINE

With the import and specialty-beer market segment growing, Coors has joined the other major breweries in developing beers to meet the demands of that market segment. These products include: Killian's Irish Red, Oktoberfest Marzen, and Winterfest.

THE MICROS

Now that you have met the giants of the United States brewing fraternity, let's turn our attention to the micro-breweries.

Today there are more than 400 micro-breweries and pub-breweries busy turning out more than 2% of the beer consumed in the United States. That doesn't sound like much, until you realize that United States breweries produce more than 200 million barrels of beer a year. There are so many breweries, and brewers, who deserve mention that it would take another book just to cite each one by name and list their products.

I have chosen to profile the following breweries because they have contributed significantly to the appreciation and growth of the micro-brewery segment of the United States beer market. (Appendix 1 in the back of this book lists at least one micro-brewery or brew-pub in each state where their existence is legal. I strongly suggest that you visit one or more. These breweries are brewing some very fine beers, as well as some that could use some improvement. It is important to remember that only by exploration can you find the best.)

ANCHOR BREWING COMPANY

1705 Mariposa Street
San Francisco, CA 94107
415-863-8350

Anchor Brewing Company has built its reputation on brewing a beer that had, until 1965, been considered inconsistent at best. The Anchor Steam Beer brewed today, the creation of Fritz Maytag and a number of other talented brewers, is considered the best of its style. The term "steam beer" (a trademark of the Anchor Brewing Company) appears to have been a local nickname for beer that was brewed in the San Francisco area in the nineteenth century. Some evidence indicates that by the turn of the century these beers would be fermented with lager yeasts. It is said that eruption of foam on tapping a keg of this sort of beer was so dramatic that it was called "steam."

As with all success stories, there is the legend and the truth. In the case of the Anchor Brewing Company, I will let Fritz Maytag separate fact from fiction:

> The real story is that in 1965, a friend who ran the Old Spaghetti Factory in San Francisco, a charming, inexpensive restaurant in the North Beach section which only served Anchor Steam on draft from the day it opened in 1957, told me that Anchor Brewery was going to close at the end of the week. They were bankrupt. He suggested that I go see it because he thought it would interest me. I have always suspected that he thought I might give them some financial help. The next morning I went, and it was love at first sight. That very day I agreed to buy the controlling interest for almost nothing.

In fact, Maytag took controlling interest in the Anchor Brewing Company in 1965. Once he bought the place he became fascinated by the brewery, and with brewing beer. In 1969 he took sole ownership of the company, totally renovated the brewing equipment, installed a bottling line for the first time in the brewery's history, and began to turn the business around. In 1979 Anchor moved to a much larger building. At the old facility, in 1977, they brewed 12,000 barrels of beer; by 1987 they were brewing 44,500 barrels.

PRODUCT LINE

Anchor Porter was introduced in 1974. Its deep, almost black color and rich flavor are the result of using roasted malted and unmalted barley, fermented with a lager yeast.

Liberty Ale was released in 1975. It is a top-fermented ale, "bunged" for natural carbonation and dry-hopped for a very aromatic nose and dry flavor.

Anchor's Special Christmas Ale: Every year since 1975, the Anchor Brewing Company has brewed a unique ale for the holiday season. It is very different every year and is available only from Thanksgiving through New Year's.

Old Foghorn has only been in major distribution since 1985. For 10 years before that, it had been brewed only in small batches for local distribution. Because of the fact that only the first "run" of wort is rich enough to build this high gravity brew, three mashes are required to produce enough wort for each barley-wine brew length. Old Foghorn is dry hopped, and is fermented with an ale yeast that, because of the high alcohol content of the beer, is unable to ferment all the sugars. The resulting sweetness, combined with the warmth of the alcohol, balances this highly hopped brew.

Anchor Wheat Beer is the latest addition to the Anchor product line. It was first brewed in 1984 to celebrate the fifth anniversary at the "new" brewery. The mash is more than two-thirds malted wheat. The wort is hopped with a variety of hops and is fermented with an ale yeast.

THE BOSTON BEER COMPANY

30 Germania Street
Boston, MA 02130
617-522-3400

The story of the founding of the Boston Beer Company is another tale of success rife with legend. The company's president, Jim Koch (pronounced "Cook"), left a career as a management consultant in 1983 to start Boston Beer with $100,000 in savings, plus $300,000 raised from family and friends.

Koch contracted the Pittsburgh Brewing Company to make a beer based on a recipe from his great-great-grandfather. There is no doubt that Koch was, and continues to be, a master of marketing. Armed with his great-great-grandfather's recipe, he solidified the perception of his beers' Colonial American heritage by naming his beers after the former governor of Massachusetts, Samuel Adams, signer of the Declaration of Independence, and beer brewer. In 1985, Koch had perfected his beer and began marketing the product door-to-door, convincing the tavern owners of Boston to carry his product.

To expand his market in 1986, Koch contracted the Oregon brewery Blitz-Weinhard, to make beer for distribution in the western United States. That same year Koch opened a pub-brewery in Philadelphia called Samuel Adams BrewHouse. In 1988, the company was able to don the mantle of "micro-brewery" by beginning operations in a renovated old brewery in Boston.

Recently, Koch has once again expanded the market for his Samuel Adams products with their introduction to the German beer market. Plans to expand further into the European market are still on tap.

PRODUCT LINE

Boston Lager has a deep golden color, rich malt body, and spicy hop flavor. Starting Gravity: 1.050. Malt: two-row Klages, Harrington Crystal. Hops: German Hallertau and Tettnang Tettnanger. Yeast: bottom-fermenting lager yeast.

Samuel Adams Boston Lager

Boston Lightship is a light beer brewed with all malt and imported hops. Starting Gravity: 1.032. Malt: two-row Klages, Harrington Crystal. Hops: Saaz, German Hallertau, and Tettnang Tettnanger. Yeast: bottom-fermenting lager yeast.

BOSTON Lightship

Samuel Adams Boston Stock Ale was first brewed to celebrate the opening of the Samuel Adams Brewery in Boston. It is a red amber ale. Starting Gravity: 1.056. Malt: two-row Klages and Harrington Crystal. Hops: Saaz, Fuggles, and Goldings. Yeast: top-fermenting ale yeast.

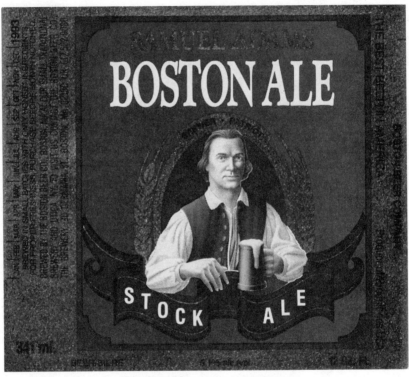

SAMUEL ADAMS BOSTON STOCK ALE

Samuel Adams Honey Porter has an almost opaque dark brown color. Starting Gravity: 1.056. Malt: two-row Klages, malted wheat, roasted barley and chocolate malt. Hops: Saaz, Fuggles, and Goldings. Yeast: top-fermenting ale yeast.

SAMUEL ADAMS HONEY PORTER

Samuel Adams Double Bock is a ruby-colored lager, styled after a Bavarian monastic bock beer (available only in late winter). Starting Gravity: 1.081. Malt: two-row Klages and Harrington Crystal. Hops: Hallertau Mittelfrueh, Tettnang Tettnanger, and Saaz. Yeast: bottom-fermenting lager yeast.

Samuel Adams Double Bock

Samuel Adams Dark Wheat is a deep brown brew made with wheat malt and roasted wheat malt (available only in late spring). Starting Gravity: 1.045–49. Malt: two-row Harrington, wheat malt, roasted wheat malt, and chocolate malt. Hops: Saaz and Tettnang Tettnanger. Yeast: top-fermenting Weihenstephan.

Samuel Adams Summer Wheat is a golden-colored brew made with wheat and barley malt (available only in summer). Starting Gravity: 1.042. Malt: malted wheat, two-row Klages, and Harrington. Hops: Saaz, Hallertau Mittelfrueh, and Tettnang Tettnanger. Yeast: top-fermenting Weihenstephan.

Samuel Adams Octoberfest is a reddish amber brew (available only in early fall). Starting Gravity: 1.042. Malt: malted wheat, two-row Klages, and Harrington. Hops: Saaz, Tettnang Hallertau, and Tettnang Tettnanger. Yeast: top-fermenting Weihenstephan.

Samuel Adams Winter Lager is a deep red amber brew (available in early winter). Starting Gravity: varies each year. Malt: two-row Klages and Harrington Crystal. Hops: Saaz, Kentish Goldings, German Hallertau, and Tettnang Tettnanger. Yeast: bottom-fermenting lager yeast.

Samuel Adams Cranberry Lambic is a light red amber brew (available in early winter). Starting Gravity: 1.040. Malt: two-row Harrington and malted wheat. Hops: Saaz and Tettnang Tettnanger. Yeast: multiple top-fermenting strains.

Samuel Adams Triple Bock is a high-alcohol-content brew fermented with both ale and champagne yeasts. Brewed with four times as much barley as used for Samuel Adams Boston Lager, this beer is sold in cobalt blue 8-ounce bottles with 24K gold lettering. Placed on the market in the winter of 1994, this brew is aiming to be the most potent beer on the market, intended to be sipped like sherry.

SIERRA NEVADA BREWING COMPANY

1075 East 20th Street
Chico, CA 95928
916-893-3520

Ken Grossman and Paul Camusi started Sierra Nevada Brewing Company in 1978. The two partners had been home brewers and, after extensive reading and research, decided to start their own micro-brewery. The design and construction of the first brewery took more than one and a half years while they both worked on other full-time jobs. The brewery, a 3,000-square-foot structure, was finished in 1980.

The original brewing equipment was constructed from used dairy equipment and other converted equipment. A used bottling line was purchased from a soft drink bottler and was converted to fit the rest of the brewing equipment. At first both Grossman and Camusi did a little bit of everything. Then they sorted out individual fields of expertise. Grossman took responsibility for daily brewing as well as plant development and maintenance. Camusi handled the fermentation and lagering of the beer, as well as quality control. He also did the bookkeeping, financial management, and product distribution.

In 1989, in order to meet demand for their products, they completed a new brewing facility. It is designed to reach an eventual capacity of 200,000 barrels annually. In October of the same year they opened a brew pub, The Sierra Nevada Taproom and Restaurant.

PRODUCT LINE

Sierra Nevada Pale Ale is a deep amber-colored brew known for its well-hopped flavor and aroma. Starting Gravity: 1.053. Malt: two-row malted barley, caramel, and dextrin malts. Hops: Perle (bittering) and Cascade (finishing). Yeast: top-fermenting ale yeast.

Sierra Nevada Pale Ale

Sierra Nevada Porter is a dark-colored, medium-bodied brew. Starting Gravity: 1.059. Malt: two-row malted barley, caramel, chocolate, black, and dextrin malts. Hops: Nugget (bittering) and Willamette (finishing). Yeast: top-fermenting ale yeast.

SIERRA NEVADA PORTER

Sierra Nevada Stout is a very dark-colored, full-bodied traditional stout. Starting Gravity: 1.070. Malt: two-row malted barley, caramel, black, and dextrin malts. Hops: Chinook (bittering) and Cascade (finishing). Yeast: top-fermenting ale yeast.

Sierra Nevada Pale Bock is a pale, very full-bodied bock-style beer (available in the spring). Starting Gravity: 1.070. Malt: two-row malted barley and dextrin malts. Hops: Perle (bittering) and Mt. Hood (finishing). Yeast: top-fermenting ale yeast.

Sierra Nevada Summerfest is a light-bodied lager with significant hop flavor and aroma (available in the summer). Starting Gravity: 1.047. Malt: two-row malted barley and dextrin malts. Hops: Perle (bittering) and Hallertau (finishing). Yeast: bottom-fermenting lager yeast.

Sierra Nevada Celebration Ale is a special full-bodied, rich beer brewed only for the winter holidays (available only seasonally). Starting Gravity: 1.070. Malt: two-row malted barley, caramel, and dextrin malts. Hops: Chinook (bittering) and Cascade (finishing). Yeast: top-fermenting ale yeast.

Sierra Nevada Bigfoot Barleywine Style Ale is a deep, reddish-brown brew that boasts a dense, fruity bouquet, and extremely rich, intense, bittersweet palate. Starting Gravity: 1.097. Malt: two-row malted barley and caramel malts. Hops: Nugget (bittering) and Cascade (finishing). Yeast: top-fermenting ale yeast.

Sierra Nevada Bigfoot Barleywine Style Ale

CHAPTER SIX
BEERS of CANADA

Although popular legend has it that Canada did not suffer a Prohibition era similar to its southern neighbor, The War Measures Act (1916–1919) successfully banned the sale of alcoholic beverages in that country. After the First World War this ban continued in all provinces except Quebec. The political makeup of Canada (a confederation of provinces with a relatively weak federal government) made the legal consumption of alcohol a patchwork quilt of "wet" and "dry" provinces, cities, and towns. Finally, in Ontario, the provincial law was changed in 1927, but some counties in that province remained dry until the late 1940s.

Today the legal patchwork quilt survives in laws that strictly govern the production and sale of beverage alcohol in Canada. In the last few years import and export differences between the various provinces (and the Canadian federal government) and the United States government have led to confrontation. At the time of this writing, these differences have been reduced to an occasional case of indigestion, with beer flowing, once again, back and forth across the border with relative ease.

The following is a brief history of the two giants of Canadian brewing: Molson and Labatt. There has been a significant interest in micro-brewing in Canada that mirrors the growth of local and regional breweries in the United States. Unfortunately, or fortunately, the growth has been such that an accurate description of the number and character of these new breweries will have to wait for another time. Limiting this chapter to the two major breweries is only an encouragement for you to seek out, and enjoy, the interesting products brewed by the rest of the Canadian breweries, large and small.

 ## LABATT BREWERIES OF CANADA

Labatt House, BCE Place
181 Bay Street (Suite 200)
Toronto, Ontario M5J 2T3 CANADA
416-361-5050

John Labatt arrived in London, Ontario, from England in 1833. He started farming and soon gained a very favorable reputation for his malting barley, which he sold to a local innkeeper's brewery. Labatt teamed up with master brewer Samuel Eccles, bought a stake in the innkeeper's operation in 1847, and began production of three brands of beer (X, XX, and XXX).

In 1854, Labatt gained full control of the brewery. Labatt died in 1866, leaving the brewery to his wife and son John II. His son modernized the company, increased production, and expanded operations as far as the Northwest Territories. By 1911 the company was incorporated as John Labatt Limited. John II died in 1915, a year before the War Measures Act was passed in Parliament. This legislation would bankrupt all but 15 of Ontario's 65 breweries. Labatt survived because of a loophole in the law that allowed the production of alcohol for export.

After World War II, Labatt went public and began a period of rapid expansion, beginning with the acquisition of Toronto-based Copland Brewing in 1946. Ten years later, W. H. R. Jarvis became the first nonfamily president of the company.

In the 1960s, Schlitz tried to acquire a 40% interest in Labatt but was blocked by U.S. antitrust regulations. By 1965 the company had a brewing capacity of 1.3 million barrels.

In 1980 the company made a deal with Anheuser-Busch to brew Budweiser in Canada, where it immediately captured about 8% of the market. With its leadership in beer intact, Labatt went on a decade-long shopping spree, acquiring an interest in the Toronto Blue Jays and several food and entertainment companies. Because Canada's antitrust laws threatened to block further Canadian expansion, Labatt began purchasing U.S. businesses, including Latrobe Brewing (Rolling Rock beer, 1987).

Today John Labatt is Canada's second largest brewer (after Molson) and the world's eighth largest beverage company. (Labatt is 38% owned by Brascan, a holding company of the Toronto branch of Canada's Bronfman family, owners of Seagram's.)

The company's share of the Canadian market inched up to 43% in 1992, largely through the strength of Labatt's Blue. Outside Canada, Labatt produces such beers as Rolling Rock in the United States (through its Latrobe subsidiary) and Birra Moretti in Italy, which contributed the lion's share of Labatt's 33% increase in European sales in 1991. Labatt also brews and sells the Budweiser and Michelob brands in Canada under license from Anheuser-Busch. Labatt brands include Birra Moretti, Budweiser (Canada), Carlsberg (Canada), Guinness (Canada), John Labatt Classic, Labatt's Blue, Labatt's Blue Light, Labatt's Dry, Labatt's Lite, Michelob (Canada), Michelob Dry (Canada), Rolling Rock, Tuborg (Canada), and Twistshandy (Canada).

MOLSON BREWERIES

175 Bloor Street East
North Tower
Toronto, Ontario M4W 3S4
CANADA
416-975-1786

John Molson was born in Lincolnshire, England. An orphan raised by his maternal grandfather, he was 18 years old when he emigrated to Canada in 1782 and arrived in Quebec City. He quickly made his way to Montreal, where he began making plans to go into the brewing business. He planned to use his inheritance and the proceeds from the sale of his father's estate in Lincolnshire, called Snake Hill, to back his business. As a minor he was faced with some legal difficulty in completing the business transactions, but by 1785, in full possession of his inheritance, he went into business and in 1786 began producing Molson's Ale.

The first Molson brewery in Montreal was on the same site as the present one, and in September 1786, its owner stood at the brewery door and paid a farmer, named Joseph Bernard, for 41 bushels of grain. Two days later Molson began malting and had hired his first assistant, Christopher Cook, for four dollars a month.

He was soon brewing other business deals as well. He invested in farms and lumber and started a foundry and a cooperage, all businesses associated with brewing. In 1808 he expanded into the transportation business by constructing Canada's first steamboat (less than one year after Robert Fulton piloted his steamboat from New York to Albany). Molson's steamboat (the *Accommodation*) was the first of a fleet that ran regular service from Montreal to Quebec City.

The Molsons, father and sons, developed their businesses through the first half of the nineteenth century. John Molson died in 1836, but his sons continued his tradition of business expansion and, in 1837, the Molson's Bank began business. It was later chartered by an act of Parliament on October 1, 1855.

Other business ventures aside, the Molson Brewing Company was not left to languish. In 1903, Molson introduced an Export Ale and by 1928 was marketing its beers in neighboring Ontario. Steady growth continued through the next two decades. In 1954, Molson Golden was brought onto the market, closely followed by Molson Canadian in 1959.

In the late 1960s the United States market was discovering imported beers, and Molson organized the Martlet Importing Company Inc. to handle exports of Molson products to the U.S. market.

Molson soon became a major player in the highly lucrative U.S. import market. In August 1989, the North American brewing operations of Molson Companies Limited joined with the Foster's Brewing Company, and Molson became Canada's largest brewery.

Today, Molson owns and operates eight breweries in seven provinces. The company produces more than 40 brands across Canada, including: Molson Canadian, Molson Special Dry, Molson Export, Miller Genuine Draft, Black Label, Coors Light, Molson Canadian Ice, Black Ice, Carling Ice, Carling Strong, Carling Light, Carling, Molson Exel, O'Keefe Ale, Old Vienna, Black Horse, and Laurentide.

THE "ICE" AGE

In a move to expand the beer market, Molson introduced "ice" beer in the Canadian market early in 1993. Based on a traditional German brewing process, the brew is chilled to subfreezing temperatures to produce ice crystals. The ice is removed, and the resulting beer is said to taste smoother. The real difference is that the beer now has a higher alcohol content. The demand for the Molson Ice swept the Canadian market and was introduced in test markets in the United States in early August 1993. By the last week of August that year Anheuser-Busch had Budweiser Ice on the U.S. market. The demand for ice beer has increased since then. Today there are more than 40 ice beers on the market in the United States and Canada.

CHAPTER SEVEN

BEERS of EUROPE

Each country in the grain belt of Europe can lay exclusive claim to at least one style of beer. England is best known for ales, Germany for lagers, and the new Czech Republic can boast of a world-class pilsner. The following discussion is a brief visit to the breweries that make these countries famous.

BEERS OF THE UNITED KINGDOM

English breweries have gone through major consolidations, similar to the shakeout that occurred in the United States in the early 1960s. The majority of beers and ales now manufactured in the United Kingdom are produced by the "Big Six": Bass, Allied Breweries, Whitbread, Watney, Courage, and Scottish & Newcastle. These companies also control a number of small local breweries that they allow to produce unique beverages for local consumption.

TIED HOUSES AND SUCH

Beer sales and distribution in the United Kingdom differs from the method used in the United States in that there is a system of "tied houses": pubs, taverns, and bars that are owned by the brewery that supplies the beers to those particular establishments. There are also "free houses" that offer beverages from many different breweries, relying mainly on the smaller local breweries to supply unique local beers and ales for their demanding customers—and British beer consumers can be very demanding.

In 1971, alarmed by the deterioration of their favorite ales, a number of people got together and formed an organization known as CAMRA (CAMpaign for Real Ale), to promote "real ale." Real ale is a traditionally produced ale that is "cask conditioned." These are ales that are neither pasteurized nor filtered before they are delivered in casks to the public house or tavern. Without preservatives, and still in intimate contact with the yeast that fermented them, these ales have a very short shelf life. If they are not consumed in a day or two, they "go off" and must be used by the publican (owner of the pub) in soups, stews, or other recipes. CAMRA continues to keep track of pubs that serve "real ale," hosts the annual Great British Beer Festival, and publishes an annual *Good Pub Guide* that lists the pubs, bars, and taverns that come up to the groups rigid standards for "good beer."

For the sake of brevity I have limited this visit to the United Kingdom to two of the best known breweries: Bass PLC, of Burton-on-Trent, and the Scottish brewery, McEwan, best known for its traditional Scottish ale.

BASS PLC

In 1777, William Bass decided to switch from transporting beer to brewing it in Burton-on-Trent, England. Burton's pure water supply allowed Bass to brew lighter ales than were being produced in London. During 1827, when barrels. In 1876, Bass became the first company to gain trademark protection (for its red triangle) under the British Trademark Registration Act of 1875. By the time of Michael Bass's death in 1884, the 145-acre Bass brewery was the largest ale and bitter brewery in the world.

Most British brewers employed the tied-house system (where breweries controlled and supplied beer to their own pubs), which limited distribution but assured them of a market for their beer. Bass instead opted for the free-trade system, selling its beer through distributors and relying for expansion on consumers' growing demand for Bass beer. The temperance movement and World War I hurt all brewers, and consumers increasingly turned to movies and other diversions instead of spending evenings at the local pub. The tied-house pubs responded by upgrading and improving their facilities to lure customers back, and Bass's sales suffered when the pubs serving its beer failed to follow suit. During the 1920s the company acquired several breweries, including the rival Worthington & Company in 1926.

When Sir James Grigg, age 70, took over in 1959, he began looking for a merger partner. Bass merged with the efficient regional brewer Mitchells & Butler in 1961. Under Sir Alan Walker, the company merged with Charrington United (Carling Black Label lager, pubs; 1967) to form a nationwide network of breweries and pubs. By 1970, Bass's British market share approached 25%. Led by lager, sales boomed.

When growth slowed in the 1980s, Bass sold its less profitable pubs and diversified, streamlining its production capacity, closing two U.K. breweries in 1991 and announcing plans to shut down two more.

Bass runs 11 breweries and more than 4,000 pubs in the United Kingdom and owns, manages, or franchises more than 1,600 hotels in more than 50 countries.

Beer Brands (U.S.): Bass, Tennent's, Worthington.

McEWAN

The William McEwan brewery was founded in 1856, then merged with the William Younger brewery to form the Scottish Brewers in 1931, which in turn underwent another merger in 1960 to become Scottish & Newcastle. Today the McEwan beers are still brewed at the McEwan site at the Fountain Brewery in Edinburgh, Scotland.

McEwan's Scotch Ale is a strong, rich, malty offering brewed for export (though it shouldn't be confused with the McEwan's Export available in Britain, which is a different brew altogether). Very dark brown in appearance, not quite opaque, it has a head that is very light tan, almost white. Its aroma has a slightly roasty tinge and is mostly a combination of malt and alcohol, which warms the sinuses, providing fair warning that this is a potent beer. In the mouth, the beer is full bodied and smooth. The taste is malty sweet and lasts for some time. The alcohol creates a warming sensation in both the mouth and the stomach. Toward the finish, the maltiness gradually gives way to this dryness, which lingers in the finish. This is a good beer for a late fall or winter evening.

BEERS OF IRELAND (REPUBLIC OF)

Any mention of brewing in Ireland must include the story of Guinness Stout. There are so many legends that have grown up around this brewery and its famous beer that I would be remiss if I did not set the record straight. The following is the true story of the development of the world's most famous stout.

GUINNESS PLC

In 1759, Arthur Guinness, at age 34, took over a small brewery at St. James Gate on the outskirts of Dublin. He leased it for 9,000 years at a annual rent of 45 pounds. Although Irish beer was almost unknown outside of Dublin, brewing was probably the fastest growing industry in Ireland at the time.

In addition to ales, Arthur Guinness brewed a beer that contained unmalted, roasted barley, which gave it the characteristically dark color and flavor of a brew that had become very popular in London a few years earlier. This brew was known as "porter" because of its popularity with the porters and stevedores of Covent Garden and Billingsgate.

Although Arthur Guinness produced a popular ale, in time he decided to develop a product that could compete with the London porters. The word "stout" was added in the early 1820s as an adjective to describe his porter. An "extra stout porter" was understood to be a stronger, more full-bodied porter. Eventually the word became the name commonly associated with the Guinness product.

GUINNESS IN A CAN?

A few years ago Guinness introduced its Guinness Pub Draft, or Guinness in a can, to the U.S. market. Prior testing in the United Kingdom and Ireland was met with marked enthusiasm, but how would beer purists in the United States take to the idea of Guinness in a can? The results have been very positive, and the only real question being asked is, "How do they do it?"

The simple, nontechnical answer is that there is a small plastic capsule filled with nitrogen secured to the bottom of the can. Since the can's contents are under pressure, some of the Guinness is forced into the plastic bladder through a pinhole. Nitrogen is used because it creates smaller bubbles than carbon dioxide and because carbon dioxide reacts with water to form carbonic acid, which can often impart a metallic taste to canned beer. Nitrogen, on the other hand, is mostly inert, and will not form an acid in water. When the can is opened, the nitrogen and beer mixture is released, creating the lovely foamy head that is the sign of a well poured Guinness.

The new Guinness Pub Draft cans are also a case of an innovative solution to an everyday problem in many pubs, bars, and taverns in the United States. Here, many bartenders don't have the time, or inclination, to take the several minutes required to pour a proper pint. The result of a "fast pour" is a very thick, rocky head, as opposed to a rich, smooth, dense head. The Pub Draft system eliminates that problem. (There is only one minor drawback. The beer must be served quite cold or, on opening, you will be wiping half the contents off the ceiling.)

BLACK AND TAN/HALF AND HALF

Black and Tan is a mixture of stout and ale. The name was also associated with the black and tan uniforms of the British soldiers who were sent to Ireland during the "Troubles" in 1918. The arrival of these soldiers was not appreciated by the people of Ireland. (For this very reason it is not a good idea to order a Black and Tan in Ireland! If you want one of these interesting combinations of Guinness and ale, ask for a "Half and Half.") In this country, a Black and Tan is poured so that the ingredients separate in the glass, presenting the customer with an amber layer of ale topped with a rich black layer of stout. In Ireland, it is not served layered. Personally, I prefer the effect of the layered drink. It makes a great conversation piece.

BEERS OF BELGIUM

For its size, Belgium has more different kinds of beers than any other country in the world. These beers are truly unique, both in their production and in their range of flavors. First of all there are the distinct Belgian styles of beer: lambic, gueuze, faro, saison, trappiste, kriek, framboise, witbier, and Abbey "single," "double," and "triple" ales.

In the past few years, the beers of Belgium have caught the attention of beer drinkers in the United States and Europe. There is no doubt that this country produces some of the most unusual beers in the world. Each of Belgium's nine provinces produces a number of beers unique to that province. A study of the history of Belgium, with a side trip into the fascinating world of famous Flemish and Waloon painters, would certainly help in making sense of the origins of many of these beers.

The following sections describe a number of unique styles particular to Belgian brewing: lambic, faro, kriek, framboise, gueuze, saisons, wit (white) beer, and monastic beers (Abbey and Trappist).

LAMBIC

Lambic is a "beer" of spontaneous fermentation, produced in the Lezze valley in Belgium. According to Belgian law, lambic can be brewed only in the region around Brussels.

The grist is made up of close to 60% unmalted barley and almost 40% malted wheat. These grains are mashed, and the resulting wort is boiled for between four and five hours. The hops used are from a strain of less bitter hop. (Traditionally, the hops are at least three years old. They are used more as a preservative than for flavor.)

The wort is then piped to an open-air vat where it is left overnight to the whims of wild yeast spores borne on the cool gusts of night air that sweep down the valley of the Zenne river. In the early morning the beer is piped into wooden barrels where a further fermentation takes place. There, yeasts identified as *Brettanomyces bruxellensis* and *Brettanomyces lambicus,* produce a relatively low alcohol beer. Lambic, either in bottle or from the cask, is a relatively still beverage; rather than carbonation, it has a slight "sparkle." For the most part, these beers are sold to make gueuze.

FARO

Faro is a young lambic that is sweetened and sometimes spiced; when bottled, it's usually pasteurized to keep the added sugar from fermenting.

FRUIT LAMBICS

Kriek

To make a real kriekenlambic, you will need a basic lambic and cherries from Schaarbeek (frowned upon by purists; you can also use *some* cherries from other regions of Belgium). The kriekenlambic must then be lagered in old German wine or Porto oak barrels. These barrels are not sealed. The bung hole is left open, and a tree branch is inserted to prevent the opening from being closed by the fermenting cherries.

Frambozenbier (Raspberry)

This beer is also based on a lambic. With the infusion of ripe, red raspberries in the secondary fermentation, the beer takes on the essence of the raspberry flavor and some of its color.

GUEUZE

Gueuze (the *g* is a "loud" *g*, as in an angry "grrr"; the *eu* is pronounced something like the *ow* in "to owe someone"; the *ze* is pronounced as in "Liza Minelli") is a mix between several lambics (younger and older): the age of the gueuze is the age of the youngest lambic used in the mixture. Blending lambics became popular because the spontaneous fermentation of the lambic leads to some unusual results. The blending of pure lambics of different ages also restarts fermentation in the keg or bottle. This second fermentation creates the carbonation in a true gueuze.

Before the First World War there were more than 300 beer merchants in Brussels who bought up stocks of lambic, young and old, to blend and make gueuze. Most of what they made was sold in the cafe that each of the merchants ran. At that time gueuze was considered the "champagne" among beers.

Today there are only about a dozen blenders who still practice the art of blending lambic into gueuze. Frank Boon is a good example of a blender who has expanded the market for gueuze into the United States.

Generally, gueuze is a clear beer with a good head and the famous Belgian lace. (Belgian lace is the pattern the head of a good beer leaves on the side of the glass as the beer is consumed.) In Brussels, some of the cafes buy their lambics and then make their own gueuze.

TRAPPIST BEERS

Trappist beers are top-fermented, bottled-conditioned, usually slightly sweet ales brewed by Trappist monks. There are only six true Trappist breweries (five in Belgium and one in the Netherlands): Chimay, Orval, Rochefort, Westmalle, and St. Sixtus at Westvleteren in Belgium, and Schaapskooi at Koningshoeven in the Netherlands. Only a beer made at a Trappist monastery can officially use the word Trappist in the name of its beer. The Belgian Triple is the strongest of the Trappist beers, but is also one of the lightest in color. It is somewhat confusing that the Double is a darker, yet weaker, beer than the Triple, which is quite light. The most amazing thing about the beer is its sweetness.

BELGIAN BREWERIES

To pick one of the hundreds of Belgian breweries as representative of the breweries of that country is difficult. Most of the breweries are small and family-run concerns. The largest are developing a corporate character that has begun to affect the otherwise unique character of their products. As a result, I have had to resort to choosing, at random, a brewery that still has a special personality and produces a range of products that roughly represent the most popular styles that are readily available in the United States. In no way does my choice leave you with an excuse not to explore the unmentioned breweries, such as the Trappist breweries mentioned earlier in this chapter. To do so would be a sin.

LIEFMANS

 Aalst Straat 200
9700 Oudenaarde,
Belgium
(055) 31.13.91

The Liefmans brewery has been brewing traditional beers of Oudenaarde. Today it is also a working museum of beer making. The brew house is made up of traditional copper mash tun, brew kettle, and cooler. It takes seven days to brew a batch of beer. Fermentation is done in open copper tanks. The bulk of Liefmans production is a brown ale called Goudenband.

Liefmans also produces a kriek (cherry) beer. It is brewed once a year, at the end of July, when the Schaarbeek cherries are harvested. After the cherries are prepared, they are added to one-year-old Goudenband to age for six or seven months. This kriekbier is then filtered and bottled. Kriekbier is not the only fruit-infused brew from Liefmans. It also produces a Frambozenbier with the addition of fresh raspberries to its Goudenband ale.

GOUDENBAND BROWN ALE

Goudenband Brown Ale is brewed with four styles of barley malt: Pils, Caravienne, Munich, and Torrified. Four varieties of hops are used: Hallertau, Brewers Gold, Saaz, and Tettnang.

Following fermentation in open vessels, Goudenband is conditioned in tanks for eight to 10 months, then bottled and racked. The beer in the bottle is a "bottle-conditioned" product. The sediment in the bottom of the bottle is the yeast that conditioned that particular bottle of beer. This beer should be stored in a cool, dark place, on its side to keep the cork moist. It should be served at cellar temperature.

Original gravity: 1.057.
Alcohol content: 5.0% by volume.

LIEFMANS KRIEKBIER

Liefmans Kriekbier is brewed once a year, when the Schaarbeek cherries are harvested in July. It takes one pound of cherries, added to each gallon of six-month-old Goudenband Brown Ale, to make one gallon of Liefmans Kriekbier. After the fruit is added to the beer, it is allowed eight months of maturation before it is filtered and bottled for conditioning in the brewery's caves. There it is aged for at least two years. Although this is a bottle-conditioned beer, the yeast has been removed by filtration so the beer will continue maturing in the bottle for only two or three years after leaving the brewery. This beer is best stored, and served, slightly chilled.

Original gravity: 1.067.
Alcohol content: 7.93% by volume.

BELGIAN TRIVIA
Oerbier and Hapkin

*An **oerbier** is, in fact, a beer that is made in a traditional way. The name of the beer means something like "beer from the dark ages."*

*A **hapkin** is a beer that may be classified within the group "Duvel, Brigand" and some other herb beers.*

BEERS OF THE CZECH REPUBLIC

With the peaceful separation of the Czech and the Slovok republics, beer lovers have had to pay close attention to their European social studies in order to keep track of where their favorite beers come from. In the past few years the town of Plzen, and the brewery of Pilsner Urquell, have once again captured the attention of beer drinkers.

PILSNER URQUELL

Although the word *pilsner* is often used to describe any pale lager beer, it actually designates the specific style of beer traditionally brewed in Plzeň, in the Czech Republic.

The pilsner style of beer can be traced back to 1842, when Franciscian monks began brewing a unique beer, using a new, bottom-fermentation method. The result was the world's first clear, golden beer, considerably different from the darker, cloudy ales that were the dominant style of beer being brewed at that time.

Because of the popularity of this new style of beer, Plzeň's brewers, who had a brewing tradition going back to 1292, joined resources and, in 1898, built a single large brewery in the city. They decided to call their beer "Pilsner Urquell," combining the name of their city with the German word for "original."

Soon new railroad routes were transporting Pilsner Urquell throughout Europe. Czech and Slovak immigrants created a demand in the United States, so that by 1914 it was one of the top-selling imported beers in this country. Unfortunately, the next 70 years were not good years for fans of this product. A couple of World Wars and a political regime that was less than friendly to the idea of a free market economy created problems for the brewery.

CHANGES IN PILSEN

One of the important steps taken by the brewery in modernizing production has been the addition of stainless steel tanks to replace traditional pitch-lined oak barrels. The brewery already uses a lot of stainless steel for aging and has recently experimented with converting from oak to stainless steel for fermenting. As of now it has decided against this. Because the aging in stainless steel did not alter the beer character, they decided to go ahead and convert the rest of their aging tanks over to stainless steel and increase the brewery's overall capacity. They will retain the open-top pitch-lined oak fermenters that they presently use.

THE "NEW" PILSNER URQUEL

Today, Pilsner Urquell is the only Czech beer in national distribution in the United States. Imported by Guinness USA, it is being marketed enthusiastically.

On Friday, September 11, 1992, at 1:00 P.M., on the West Balcony of Grand Central Station in New York City, the ceremonial "first keg" of Pilsner Urquell to be imported into the United States under agreement with the Guinness Import Company was tapped and enjoyed. The usual plethora of public relations and advertising people enjoyed the fact that the presentation was going off without a hitch. The brew masters from the Pilsner Urquell Brewery looked less than comfortable with all the attention. When they were asked if there had been any changes in the beer to adapt it to "American" tastes, they were very candid. Through an interpreter, it was confirmed that the beer had been subtly changed to allow it to be transported such long distances without spoiling. It was also confirmed that the changes had only to do with what was already in the beer. Reaction has been mixed. An astute taster will note that the hop aroma and flavor are stronger than in the past.

BUDWEISER BUDVAR

There are two "Buds" in this world. One is the King of Beers that is brewed in St. Louis, Missouri. The other, called Budweiser Budvar, is brewed by the Budvar brewery in Ceske Budejovice, Bohemia, Czech Republic. And, yes, they have a "history."

The nineteenth century found the town of Ceske Budejovice (then called Budweis), once the home of the Royal Bohemian court, quietly brewing a local pilsner-style lager that became quite popular in the area. When Adolphus Busch, the soon-to-be beer magnate of St. Louis, visited that town on a trip through Europe to study the production of beer, he was so impressed that in 1876 he began brewing a pilsner-style light-colored beer just like that brewed back in Budweis. He called it Budweiser. (A good businessman, he took out a copyright on "Budweiser" as a brand name.) The brand, and Anheuser-Busch's growth was, in great part, based on the popularity of Budweiser over the heavier, darker beers of the day. Promoted as the "King of Beers" (an allusion to the royal brewery in Bohemia), the brand has now found its way into the European market.

At this point, the battle for the name "Budweiser," the lucrative import beer market of the United States, and the thirsty European Community has not moved beyond the "cold war" stages. Although no Czech Budvar Budweiser is available in the United States, stay tuned for further developments.

BEERS OF GERMANY

With the unification of Germany, the beer scene in that part of Europe changed dramatically. Most of the breweries in the area once called West Germany are high-tech plants that have honed the art and science of brewing to a razor-sharp edge. The breweries in what was once East Germany are, for the most part, less developed and produce beers of respectable quality.

THE BAVARIAN "SLEEPER"

Since this book is meant as an introduction to the world of beers, I would like to take this opportunity to introduce you to a German beer that not many people outside of Bavaria know about: wheat beer, or as it is called in the beer halls of Bavaria, "Weizenbier."

Perhaps the most famous German beer-producing region is Bavaria and, in particular, the city of Munich. There are six major breweries in Munich: Augustinerbrau, Spatenbrau, Paulanerbräu, Hacker-Pshorr Bräu, Hofbräuhaus and Löwenbräu. All of these breweries produce a range of beers, such as Pils, Export, Weizen, Hefe-Weizen, Dunkel Weizen, Marzen, and Maibock. They also produce an Oktoberfest beer for the traditional fall celebration that takes place annually in the Terressiengarten to celebrate the marriage of the Princess Terressa to the Crown Prince of Bavaria. The citizens liked the original wedding party so much that they have continued celebrating it, with only a few politically induced cancellations, since 1810.

WEIZENBIER

There are two major types of Weizenbier: Klares, or clear (without yeast), and Hefe. The Klares beers are usually served with lemon to give them a bit of tang. The Hefes should be enjoyed without it, because the lemon tends to drive the yeast to the bottom. You want the yeast to be a featured part of the flavor. In essence, a properly poured Hefe beer should be cloudy and cool—just like a fall day in Munich. There also are several subvarieties of Weizenbier—most notably dunkles (dark).

Wheat—Bavarian Hefe Weizens

In fifteenth-century Bavaria, the Dengenberger clan claimed exclusive right to brew weissbier in the Bavarian Forest and Bohemia. This lucrative monopoly fell into the hands of the Bavarian house of Dukes, when the head of the Dengenbergers failed to produce an heir. Then Maximilian I declared that the brewing of weissbier was an exclusive right of the house of Dukes, and banned public weissbier brewing, ensuring that weissbier remain a royal quaff. All was well for four hundred years or so. Then the style began to fall out of favor.

The savior of the weissbier style of beer, which is now an integral part of Bavarian life, was George Scneider. When the rights to brewing weissebier came up for renewal in 1872, George Scneider was there with his money and a pen to sign on the dotted line. Within seven years, weissebier had made a dramatic comeback in Munich, and in Bavaria. Although the "new" golden pilsner beer took some of the public acclaim, weissebier was going to survive. Today there are almost 190 breweries producing weizenbier in Bavaria and Austria.

This beer's popularity has also been boosted since the earlier days by its reputation as a tonic or even a medicine. Health-conscious beer connoisseurs make sure that the yeast has not been filtered out; many Bavarian brewers point out that this vital ingredient has not been removed by indicating it is Hefe-Weizen (wheat beer with yeast). The ale yeast is removed and a lager culture is added at bottling for bottle conditioning so that the yeast flocculates better.

WEIZEN TRIVIA

The plural of Weizen is Weizen.

Kristallklares Weizen is often called Kristallweizen.

THE BEERS OF DENMARK

Any book about beer would be incomplete without explaining the difference between "ale" and "lager" yeast. Any mention of yeast would be incomplete without the mention of *Saccharomyces carlsbergensis*. Any mention of *Saccharomyces carlsbergensis* would be incomplete without a visit to the brewery where that yeast was discovered.

 ## CARLSBERG AS

Copenhagen-based Carlsberg is the third largest brewer in Europe and the fourteenth largest worldwide. The company's beers, sold primarily under the Carlsberg and Tuborg labels, control Denmark's beer market. The company also maintains licensing agreements with such industry leaders as Labatt and Anheuser-Busch.

The modern Carlsberg AS stems from the merger of two Danish breweries. The first, Carlsberg, was established in 1847 in Copenhagen by Captain J. C. Jacobsen. Tuborg, the second great Danish brewing enterprise, was founded as Tuborgs Fabrikker in 1873 by a group of Danish businessmen who wanted to establish a major industrial project on a piece of land around Tuborg Harbor.

After World War II both launched an intense marketing plan to carry their beers outside Denmark, establishing breweries in Europe and Asia. This drive by both brewers to establish markets in foreign countries greatly influenced their decision to merge. In 1970 the two companies joined together under the name of United Breweries, but reverted to the old Carlsberg name in 1987. Carlsberg is brewed and marketed in the United States and Canada under license to Anheuser-Busch (1985) and John Labatt (1988).

BEERS OF THE NETHERLANDS

There is no doubt that Heineken is a brand that is well known to almost every beer drinker in the United States. Imported since the repeal of Prohibition, it remains the largest selling import in the United States today. The story of how this came to happen is one of the most interesting chapters in the history of the company now known as Heineken NV.

 HEINEKEN NV

In 1864, Gerard Heineken bought the 270-year-old De Hooiberg (The Haystack) brewery in Amsterdam. In 10 years he also established a brewery in Rotterdam. During the 1880s and early 1890s the company perfected the yeast strain (Heineken A-yeast) that it still uses in its beer today.

In 1914, Heineken passed the company down to his son Dr. Henri Pierre Heineken, who decided to expand the company's operations to the United States. While on the sea voyage across the Atlantic Ocean, Heineken met Leo van Munching, a bartender on the ship. Recognizing van Munching's talent, Heineken hired him to be the company's U.S. importer. After Prohibition was repealed, Heineken was the first foreign beer to reenter the U.S. market.

Following World War II, Heineken sent his son Alfred to learn the business under van Munching. While in New York, Alfred mastered the art of advertising and marketing and brought his new skills home with him in 1948. Meanwhile in the United States, van Munching created a national distribution system.

In 1968, Heineken bought the Amstel Brewery in Holland (founded in 1870), and two years later the company became a producer of stout through the acquisition of James J. Murphy in Cork, Ireland. In 1988 the company launched Buckler, a nonalcoholic beer, which has since risen to take the number two spot worldwide for nonalcoholic brews. In 1991 the company bought the Van Munching U.S. import business.

Today, Amsterdam-based Heineken, the leader in the Dutch beer market, is the third largest beer producer in the world (after Anheuser-Busch and Miller) and the largest in Europe. Heineken is the number one imported beer in the United States, and the company's Amstel Light is the leading U.S. imported light beer.

CHAPTER EIGHT

INTERNATIONAL BEERS

BEERS OF AUSTRALIA

The seminal image of Australia and beer, for those of us in North America, was the introduction of the "Foster's" pilsner-style lager in a 740 ml (25 oz.) can. Dubbed the "Oil Can," this light-flavored, effervescent beer became the "party" beer in the mid 1970s. It remains a popular beer today, even though it is now brewed just across the border in Canada.

American beer drinkers began their love affair with Foster's when they discovered that it was an "imported" beer that tasted like "American" beer. Best of all, it came in a huge red, blue, white, and gold-colored "beer drinkers sized" can. The Oil Can quickly became an Australia icon with an image ably enhanced by the antics of the comedy group "Monty Python" and the heroics of the actor Paul Hogan in the *Crocodile Dundee* movies.

The following is a brief history of the Foster's Brewing Company Ltd., as rough-and-tumble as any Paul Hogan movie!

FOSTER'S BREWING GROUP LTD.

In 1839, Scotsman Alexander Lang Elder arrived at what would become Port Adelaide, Australia, and founded Elder Smith Goldsborough, a trading company to serve local farmers. Over the next 140 years his company grew into one of Australia's largest commodities trading and farm services companies. But it did not achieve international notoriety until the early 1980s, when it became a takeover target for Robert Holmes a Court, then reputed to be Australia's richest man.

Elder Smith turned to John Elliott, managing director of Henry Jones (IXL), a Tasmanian jam and food company. (The name *IXL* was coined by the company's semiliterate founder to mean "I excel.") Elliott suggested that Elder Smith take over Henry Jones (IXL) to thwart Holmes a Court, and the companies became Elders IXL in 1981. Then in 1983, Carlton and United Breweries (CUB), which owned 49% of Elders, was also threatened by a takeover. (CUB had been founded in 1888 by brothers W. M. and R. R. Foster. The company had first exported its Foster's Lager in 1901 to serve Australian forces fighting the Boer War. By 1986 the lager was sold in 80 countries.)

In two days Elliott raised $720 million and captured more than half of the brewery (buying the rest in 1984), making Elders one of Australia's largest companies.

In 1989, Elliott and other Elders executives launched a $4.4 billion management takeover that netted about 50% of Elders. In 1990, Elliott stepped down as CEO and became nonexecutive deputy chairman. His replacement, Peter Bartels, launched a major restructuring in which the company changed its name to Foster's Brewing Group and sold off all of its nonbrewing assets. In 1991, Foster's purchased the brewing interests of Grand Met in exchange for Foster's 50% interest in Courage Pubs. Also in 1991, Foster's introduced Canada's first low-alcohol beer, Molson Exel.

THE BEERS OF ASIA

Although there are a number of breweries in the Pacific rim that are major players in that market, only the Japanese breweries have taken a major interest in the United States market. One of the most active has been Kirin Brewery Company, Ltd.

KIRIN BREWERY COMPANY, LTD.

American William Copeland arrived in Yokohama in 1864 and, five years later, established the Spring Valley Brewery, the first in Japan to provide beer for the foreign nationals on the island. Lacking funds to continue the enterprise, Copeland closed the brewery in 1884. One year later a group of thirsty foreign and Japanese businessmen reopened it as the Japan Brewery. This business created the Kirin label in 1888 and was soon turning a profit. Initially, the company was predominantly operated by Americans and Europeans, but by 1907 the Japanese had taken full control and had adopted Kirin as the company name. The mythical *kirin* is a half-horse, half-dragon creature that is said to bring good fortune to those lucky enough to see it.

After World War II, the U.S. occupation forces inadvertently assisted Kirin when they split Dai Nippon Brewery (Kirin's main competitor) into two companies (Asahi and Sapporo) while leaving Kirin intact. Kirin established itself as Japan's leading brewer during the 1950s.

The company made rapid technological advances in the 1960s when it developed superior strains of malting barley and learned new ways to control the fermentation process. A member of the Mitsubishi *keiretsu* (business group), Kirin is a recognized leader in brewing technology, having brought the industry its Amagi-Nijo malting strain, now used in more than half of the world's beer.

The company's near-50% Japanese market share in beer seems impressive, but in 1986 this share was about 60% until new products from other breweries (such as Asahi's dry beer) stole a hefty percentage of Kirin's business. In 1990, Kirin released Ichiban Shibori, a beer made, unusually, from the first wort, or press, in the brewing process. Kirin hopes to repeat this success with its Akiaji (which means "autumn taste," a beer geared to autumn demand) and Kirin Premium Beer (a high-quality brand).

CHAPTER NINE

How to Serve Beer

Beer, even that produced by a mega-brewery, is a rather delicate product. It has three enemies: age, heat, and light. Whether you keep beer for your own consumption at home or patronize retailers or restaurants, the care of beer is the same.

The most essential thing to remember about serving beer is that it should be the freshest beer you can get. This is important whether you are enjoying that beer in your home or purchasing it in a bar, tavern, or restaurant.

In the best of all possible worlds, the ideal way to ensure that you are getting a fresh beer is to find a local micro-brewery or brew pub and visit it often. In the real world we are not able to do that as often as we would like. We have to make a little effort to ensure we can find good beer.

To begin with, it is important to deal only with retailers and wholesalers who take care of their beer. A good wholesaler should make every effort to ensure that their stock is constantly rotated so that old beer is returned to the supplier and not sold to their accounts. Beer that has been kept in a warehouse where the temperature gets above 80°F, or is left out in the sun during any phase of shipping, can deteriorate. This result is "off" flavors, a metallic flavor, or a "cardboard" flavor. None of these flavors is appropriate for a beer. Beer that is nonpasteurized (cold filtered) or bottled with live yeast is especially susceptible to temperature spoilage.

A good retailer should know the wholesaler and deal only with a supplier who takes care of the beer sold to his or her accounts. It is also important that a good retailer follow the same rules as his or her wholesaler. The retailer should keep a close eye on inventory control and customer demand. Beer that doesn't sell should be returned to the wholesaler or sold at cost to get it off the shelves.

It is also important to keep beer, especially the products of breweries that don't pasteurize their beer, well chilled. The ideal situation is for beer to be kept at close to 50°F, but that is seldom possible, so standard refrigeration is often the only alternative to keeping beer out on the "floor." A knowledgable retailer will keep as much inventory as possible in the cold box to ensure it will stay as fresh as possible for as long as possible.

The third important aspect of keeping beer fresh it to protect it from sunlight or fluorescent light. Light can react with the hop oils in beer and cause the beer to go "skunky." This is especially true of beers that are bottled in green glass bottles: Heineken, Moosehead, and Molson. Brown glass bottles protect the hop oils from the particular wavelength of light that causes "off" flavors.

Retailers appreciate customers who can ensure a demand for beers that sell at a relatively high margin. It is a good idea to get together with a number of your friends, find a reliable retailer, and make arrangements to ensure that if he or she can provide beers that you like, especially "special" beers, you will keep those beers moving off the shelves. That is good business for both of you.

NOW IT'S UP TO YOU

After you have found a retailer who can consistently provide you with fresh beer, it is up to you to present that beer, at your table, to your friends, in the most appropriate way.

Drinking beer straight from the bottle is fine for camping trips, softball games, or other instances when the refreshment of a cold, wet beverage is the reason for drinking beer. To bring out all the nuances of a good beer, however, it should be served properly. There are three important aspects to serving beer properly: temperature, glassware, and how the beer is poured.

Lagers, ales, and specialty beers such as lambic or rauch beer should be poured at a temperature that brings out the flavors of the malt, hops, and essential esters created by the yeast. As a general rule, darker beers (and beers fermented at warmer temperatures) should be served as close to cellar temperature (50°F) as possible. Lighter-colored beers, especially lager beers (fermented at cold temperatures), can be served between 40 and 50°F. The reason is that the fermentation process creates special flavors that can be appreciated only at temperatures close to fermentation temperatures. You should *never* serve a beer colder than 40°F. Temperatures this cold mask all flavor and the only sensation you will experience is the refreshing sparkle of a carbonated beverage.

BEER-CLEAN GLASSES

As with any well-prepared food or graciously presented wine, beer should be a joy for the eye as well as for the palate. This means that it should be served in a "beer-clean" glass that is appropriate for the particular style of beer.

A waiter's trick I once heard of involved the problem of keeping champagne from foaming over the side of the champaign flute when pouring for customers at their table. The waiters told me that if they ran their finger lightly around the lip of the flute, there would be enough natural oil left on the glass to keep the wine from bubbling over the edge of the glass. The same trick holds true for pouring beer. There is nothing like a spot of oil, grease, or lipstick to knock the head of a beer flat. That is why good bars, taverns, pubs, and restaurants never wash their beer glasses in the same dishwasher as the rest of the dishes, glassware, or cutlery. Beer glasses should be washed only in a separate sink, first in hot water with detergent, then rinsed well in cool water and left to air dry. Only then should they be polished with a clean, lint-free dish towel. All of this process assures that there are no oils or particles of dust on the glasses to cause heads to fall or bubbles to coat the sides of the glass. Any particle of dust that is allowed to stay on the inside of a glass will catch bubbles and create a sheet of bubbles to cling to the inside of the glass when the beer is poured. If the beer is being dispensed from a draft tap, there is also a specific technique for pouring draft beer. The proper way to serve draft beer can be seen in the illustration on pages 126–127, thoughtfully provided by the Interbrew of Belgium. No matter the source—keg, cask, or bottle—a perfectly poured glass of beer is a joy to behold.

If the beer is being poured from a bottle, the first few ounces should be poured directly down into the bottom of the glass and allowed to create a thick, rich head. Then the glass should be tipped slightly, and the beer should be allowed to flow down the inside of the glass rapidly, but not so fast that you end up with half a glass of beer and half a glass of foam.

A properly poured lager beer should have about an inch or so of head, and the carbonation should rise directly from the bottom of the glass. Ales often have less head because they are less carbonated. Stouts should be poured so that they have just a quarter of an inch of head. (This is a legal requirement when serving Guinness in the Republic of Ireland, as it has been determined that the head on Guinness is essential to the full enjoyment of the product.)

TYPES OF GLASSES

The shape of the glass should enhance the style of beer that has been poured. Pilsner should be poured into a tall pilsner glass so that the carbonation can dance from the bottom of the glass all the way up to the rich white head that graces the top of the beer. Porters, stouts, and ales can be served in either straight-sided pint glasses or dimpled pub mugs. Each and every Belgian beer has a specific glass just for that beer. The illustration on pages 128–129 shows a selection of Belgian beer glasses emblazoned with the name of the beer that should be served in each of them. (It came as a surprise to me when I also found out that each and every Belgian beer can be matched to a specific cheese that should be served with it—but that's another story.)

ORDERING BEER IN A RESTAURANT

THE BEER

Fresh beer, preferably on draft, is absolutely necessary to its drinkers' enjoyment. Three things ensure a fresh-tasting brew: sufficient turnover (supplies of draft and bottled beer cannot be allowed to linger in the cooler or in the cellar); a consistent supply of fresh beer (beer in shipping containers left in the sun for days can be ruined before it gets to the retailer or tavern); and, in the case of a restaurant, tavern, or bar, a manager/owner and staff who know how to treat beer properly (store in a cool dark place and serve at the proper temperature).

GLASSES

Is the glassware "beer clean"? (Glasses and mugs washed in soap or in a dishwasher, will pick up a film that kills a beer's

THE RIGHT WAY TO TAP BEER

1

Use the correct branded glass, clean it with detergent and rince it before draughting.

2

Open the tap in one quick action, and let the first drop of beer flow away.

3

Pour the beer into the glass, by holding it at 45°, just under the tap, but do not let the tap touch the glass and do not dip it into the beer.

4

Allow the natural creation of the foam head by lowering the glass.

5

Close the tap in one quick action and move the glass away from the tap to prevent any drips falling into the beer.

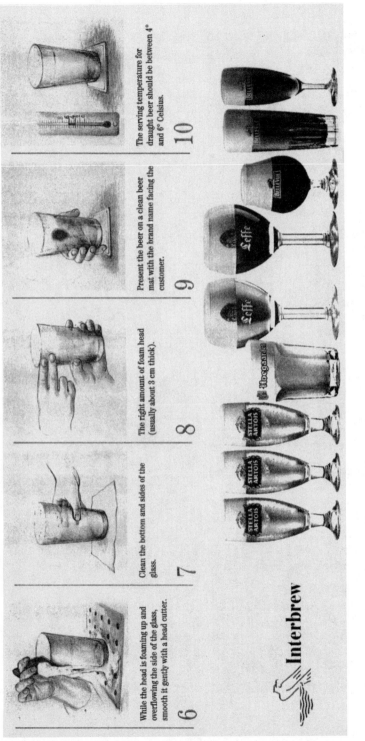

6 While the head is foaming up and overflowing the side of the glass, smooth it gently with a head cutter.

7 Clean the bottom and sides of the glass.

8 The right amount of foam head (usually about 3 cm thick).

9 Present the beer on a clean beer mat with the brand name facing the customer.

10 The serving temperature for draught beer should be between 4° and 6° Celsius.

Interbrew

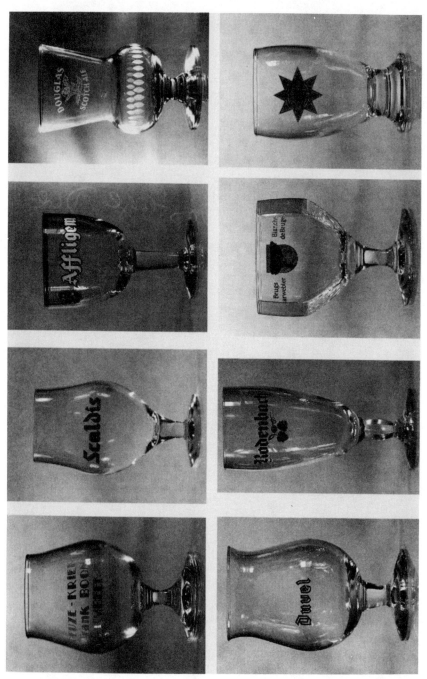

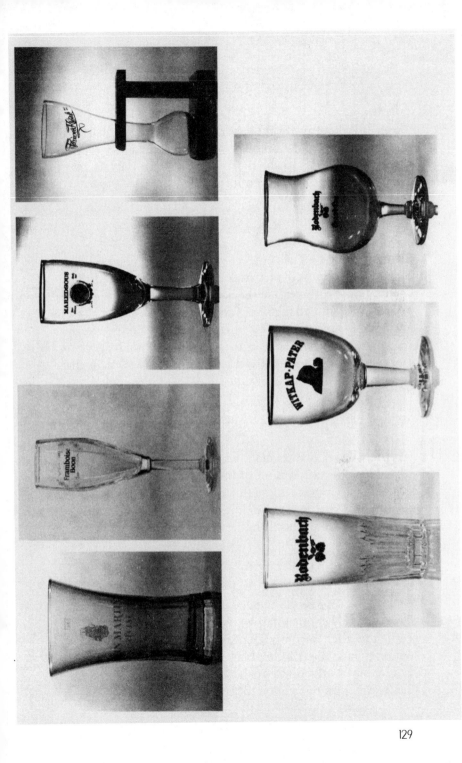

"head.") Is there an effort to use the proper shape of glassware for a particular type of beer? Pilsner beers should be served in tall, slender glasses to show off the clarity and bubbles. Ales should be served in wide-mouth glasses to enhance the aroma.

FOOD

One of the best enhancements to good beer is good food. It should be tasty, well prepared, and reasonably priced. The menu should complement the beers served. In short, the food should fit. A limited menu is a good sign. First of all, it allows the establishment to offer a "signature" dish specifically matched to the best beer in the house. The other reason is freshness. As with beer, fresh produce is the sure sign that someone cares about quality.

SERVICE

Do the staff really care about what they are doing? Does the bartender offer a selection of beers, rather than waiting for customers to request a brand name? When you ask, "What's good today?" the staff should be able to tell you the freshest beer on tap or in the bottle rather than delivering a blank stare.

THE "ENCORE EFFECT"

Ambience goes beyond the decor, the menu, and good beer. There should be something special that creates a loyal clientele. I call this the "encore effect." This is the most subjective requirement. Most of the places mentioned in this book will be places you will visit more than once, be it a month or a year before the spirit moves you to return.

CHAPTER TEN

BEER TASTING

Once again we find ourselves sharing terms and techniques with our friends from the wine world. For ages they have been taking great pleasure in tasting each and every vintage and passing judgment on it. Of course, they get to do it every new vintage, and with the wines from every vineyard in the world. All that wine and so little time!

Well, beer lovers take heart! We are about to do the same thing. The technique of seriously "tasting" beer is (in the appreciation of flavor, mouth feel, and color assessment), identical to the traditional process of tasting wine, with one exception: you don't spit. You *never* spit good (or even bad) beer into a convenient "spit bucket." There is a valid reason for this. Tasting beer uses all of your senses, and the sinus cavity is where some of the aromas resonate. The only way to incorporate the sinus cavities is to swallow the beer. Cheers!

THE BASICS OF TASTING BEER

As you have discovered in reading Chapter 4, "Styles of Beer," there are specific characteristics to each of the different styles. If a beer is to be considered an example of a particular style, it must have certain specific characteristics. Within certain parameters, there is a large area of flavors and intensity of both flavor and aroma, that makes each style the home of many different beers.

A quick review of the basic ingredients of beer is called for at this time. All beer is composed of malted barley, hops, water, and yeast. In creating a flavor perception, the two most obvious flavors are going to be the sweetness of the malt and the bitter flavor from the hops. Let's take the malt flavor first.

MALT

Although all malted barley is basically sweet, there are many different variations on the flavor that malt gives to a beer. The first difference between malts is the degree to which the malt had been roasted. The basic brewer's malt is lightly roasted (if at all) and gives the beer a sweet flavor, a very slight hint of color, and almost no aroma. The next step is into the various "crystal" and other lightly roasted malts. These give the beer more color and a flavor very much like caramel sugar. The reason is that when the malt is prepared for roasting, it is once again soaked in water (as it was when it went through the initial malting process), and this causes some of the enzymes that are still in the grain to begin to convert the outside of the starchy grain kernel to sugar. When the malt is then roasted at a relatively high temperature, this sugar is crystallized. As with any sugar syrup or even grains of cane sugar that are heated, there is a slight change in color. Lightly roasted malts also impart a slightly "nutty" aroma.

The length of the roasting process and the temperature are important in controlling the color that the roasted grain will give to the beer. In malts roasted for a short time, at low temperatures, the sugar content is relatively low and the starches and enzymes are available, after being crushed in the milling process, to be converted into maltose when mashed.

The longer the roasting and the higher the temperature, the darker the color imparted by the grain to the finished brew. For beers such as stout or porter, which both use highly roasted malt, the color is almost black and almost opaque. To get the unique flavor of stout the brewer might even use unmalted barley, kilned (roasted) until it is almost burnt. This adds unique color and flavor texture to that style of beer.

As you can see, the flavors from the malt can range from a lightly sweet flavor all the way to a rich, almost charcoal flavor. These are the basic "sweet" flavors needed to balance the bitter flavor and floral aroma of hops.

HOPS

Hops come in many different varieties. As you read in Chapter 4, different brewers use different varieties of hops. The brewers of Burton-on-Trent prefer the flavors of Kent hops for bittering their ales, while the brewers of Plzeň, in the Czech Republic have the aromatic hops of Saaz with which to finish their lagers. In the United States the brewers of the West Coast have long had a love affair with the Cascade hops of Oregon, while the brewers of the mega-brews have succeeded in blending hops until their flavors just nip at the senses. Each variety has a particular bitter flavor as well as an individual aroma. These two characteristics are important to remember when tasting a beer. The flavor of a particular hop may not quite match the initial aromatic sensation you receive when you first sample the bouquet that rises from the rich head of a perfectly poured glass of beer.

This concert of the bitter flavor and floral aroma from the hops, when combined with the sweet and, sometimes, astringent, flavors of the malts used in a beer, are also influenced by the flavors created by the specific yeast used to ferment it.

YEAST

To review the effects of yeast on the flavor of the finished beer, we recall the basic differences between ale (top-fermenting) yeast and lager (bottom-fermenting) yeast. The ale yeast ferments at higher temperatures, at a faster rate, than lager yeast. This causes the creation of esters, those aromas of apple, pear, and prune that often intrigue the olfactory senses when enjoying a good, fresh ale. On the other hand, the clean, almost grassy aromas that are integral to the enjoyment of a cool lager are also the by-product of the yeast used to ferment the golden-colored beer.

WATER

Water has much less to add to the flavor of beer than the obvious contributions of malt, hops, and yeast. Nevertheless, the mineral content of the water used to brew a specific beer has an effect on the flavor of that beer. A hard water will enhance the hop flavors. A good example of the effect of hard water on hops is the flavor of a fresh Bass ale. Soft water might add a slightly saline flavor, similar to the flavor of a sparkling mineral water.

THE BASICS OF CONDUCTING A TASTING

The fun of "blind" tasting will be covered later. For now we will concentrate on setting up a tasting of a specific style of beer.

The essential task is to get fresh bottles of beer. A little trial and error is called for here. Get to know a few retailers in your area who specialize in stocking unique beers. Keep in mind the points that were covered in Chapter 9, on the care and handling of beer. A retailer who carries hundreds of beers and keeps them in a warm window display or in a hot cellar would not be my idea of a good source of beer. A retailer who handles a quarter of that selection but cares for every bottle in a refrigerator that is set to 50°F and protects the bottles from fluorescent light and sunlight is a merchant I would get to know. If you have trouble finding a retailer who takes care of his or her beer, you might call a local micro-brewery and ask whom they use to distribute their beer, or if they could suggest a retailer who carries their products. Once you have a source for fresh, well-handled beer you can get ready to hold a tasting.

THE TASTING

The most important thing to remember about setting up a beer tasting is that it should be fun. Of course, there is a serious side to learning about the craft of brewing beer and appreciating a well-brewed beer, but the only real reason to go to all the trouble of setting up a tasting is to enjoy good beer with good friends. Sharing your impressions of beers and even keeping notes, so that you know what you liked and did not like about a beer, can become a regular event among beer afficionados. It is actually a lot more fun than just sitting around drinking for effect—especially the next morning.

With a little organization and preparation, a beer tasting is really quite simple to set up. There are a few things you must have on hand before you can run a good beer tasting: fresh beer, clean glasses, and enough notepads and pencils or pens for those who want to keep notes.

Since you will be evaluating beers for the following characteristics—appearance, bouquet, taste, aftertaste, and overall impression—you should present the beers to their best advantage. This means having enough "beer clean" glasses on hand for everyone taking part. If you do not have a massive collection of glasses so that each beer is served in the glass specifically designed for it, the best glasses to use are what are called "red wine" or "burgundy" glasses. These glasses have large bowls with relatively small mouths. This is important, because you might want to warm a selection with your hands to bring out a hop aroma; or by handling only the stem, you can keep a pilsner-style beer cool. The slightly narrow mouth helps to concentrate the aromas in the glass for easier identification. Moreover, the thin walls of the wine glass allow you to appreciate the color of the beer. One last thing about glasses: the illustration on pages 128 and 129 shows all the different glasses that go with particular styles of beers. Although it is usually important to enjoy, say, a lambic in a thistle glass or a pilsner in a tall pilsner flute, when you are tasting beers for evaluation it is more important that evaluations be standardized. Since you will eventually be tasting many different styles of beers, it is necessary that you experience the beers and not the glasses. The red wine glass has all the important characteristics that you need to concentrate on the beer and not lose any of the nuances of the flavor, aroma, or appearance of the brew you are tasting.

THIS SOUNDS PRETTY SERIOUS!

I suggest that your first few tastings be fairly well organized so that you get acquainted with the techniques of evaluation. Those of you from the world of wine will need no introduction to basic tasting techniques, but there is one important difference: in beer tasting you have to swallow!

Now that you have a good selection of friends gathered, fresh beers, and enough beer-clean glasses, I suggest you gather enough paper and pens or pencils for everyone to make a full page of notes on each beer. Now you are ready to begin.

You can have either a selection of four or five beers in the same style, or four or five beers from as many different styles.

A tasting of one style of beers allows you to concentrate on the particular beer that is considered the epitome of the style as it compares with the others. A tasting of a number of styles should start with the lightest style and progress through to the darkest, highest-alcohol style. This way you don't shock your taste buds with a high-alcohol, dark beer and then try to sense the subtleties of a light pilsner. Your taste buds will not appreciate this and, in the long run, neither will you.

First pour about three ounces of the beer you will be tasting into each glass. (Make sure you have enough beer for everyone!) The first step is to look at the beer and check its appearance. The color of the beer tells you a lot about it. A light-colored beer should have a light and malty flavor, with a slightly hoppy aroma and relatively low alcohol content. An amber color tells you that the flavor will be richer than a pale beer, but not as rich as a dark porter or stout. The almost opaque color of a stout or porter most often means you will be tasting a very hearty brew.

The aroma of the beer will confirm what your eye tells you. The surprise here might be a rich malt aroma or a spicy aroma of alcohol. (Yes, the warmth of alcohol can be sensed through smell.) Now is the time to enjoy the various hop aromatics that should be present in proper amounts for the style you are tasting. Those other aromas of apples, pears, prunes, pineapple, or vanilla are sure signs that you are about to enjoy an ale (remember that ale yeasts add a number of aromatic esters to the fermentation process).

Now it is time to sip a few ounces and enjoy the flavor and feel of the beer. The flavor should agree with the aromas, and the "mouth feel" (thin, medium, rich, or thick) should match the style of beer you are tasting. If it does not coincide with the style that it "should" be and you like it, note that it is "not to style" and enjoy it anyway.

Next, it is time to swallow, then take a quick "sip" of air, and feel the flavors and aromas of the beer resonate in the back of your throat and up into your nasal passages. You should now be experiencing the "aftertaste" for which beer is justly famous. This sensation is often overlooked after the earlier tactile excitement of seeking the most obvious various flavors and aromas, but take a moment and linger a while to enjoy this "last kiss."

If you and your friends are methodical and keep notes, you will soon have quite a library of tasting notes that will stand you in good stead when you have the opportunity to try something new. This library of flavors and aromas will help you appreciate almost any beer and truly enjoy a well-made beer.

BLIND TASTING

This is when things get really interesting. You select a style and then taste a number of beers from that particular style and rank them against each other. You are going to taste similar beers and rank them according to how they fit a specific profile. No one should know which beer is being tasted at any time. It is best to select beers that have identical bottles or to wrap the bottles in something that obscures the identity of the beer. Numbers or letters of the alphabet should be used to designate the beer being tasted. A very methodical presentation should keep slip-ups to a minimum.

This sort of tasting can often conclude with surprising results. Beers that are often dismissed because of brand name associations often score very well when tasted context with more "prestigious" beers.

CHAPTER ELEVEN

BEER AND Food

I'll be honest with you, this is my favorite chapter in this book. Here is where I got a chance to talk to some of the most exciting chefs and restaurateurs in the country about cooking and food.

This chapter is divided into conversations with the chefs. As we meet each chef, I will tell you about his particular topic of interest, his restaurant, and a little of his background. I hope you have as much fun reading this as I had researching it.

BEER AND CAVIAR

Chef Rick Moonen is executive chef and co-owner of Oceana in New York City. He has been executive chef at the Water Club and one of the founders of the Chefs and Cuisiners Club, both in New York City. Chef Moonen and I got together one Saturday afternoon to brew a batch of pale ale and chat about food. He started out with some general comments on beer.

Wine, especially vintage wine, is like making a movie. You make it and there it is. If it was a good year you have good wine, if it was a not-so-good year you end up with not-so-good wine. Beer, in contrast, is a "Broadway production." The brew master has to make sure that every batch is to "style" and is consistent in hundreds of different ways. There is no room for the brewmaster to say, "Oh well, this just wasn't a good batch." He has to be "on" every time. That's why I really have a lot of respect for beer and brewers.

Beer doesn't get the respect that wine has, and in many cases the beer is more complex than some wines. Rodenbach is a good example. Sometimes I will pour a glass for someone and ask them what grapes were used. They will actually begin to pick varietals and wonder how they were blended.

When it come to combining food and wine, Chef Moonen told me that he learned from working with wine how to bring beer to the dinner table, and that both contrast and harmony are the two keys to matching beer to food. For instance, yeast and yeast, the combination of beer and pizza. It's a classic, and it works so much better than with a wine.

He also pointed out that beer is a refreshing beverage and a classic pallet cleanser. The bitterness of the hops is perfect for cleansing the pallet of stronger tasting foods. Chef Moonen then had a surprise for me.

A good example of how beer works with stronger tasting food is pairing beer and caviar. A good dry pilsner beer with caviar is a perfect match. The traditional match of cavier and champagne is really overkill. Many people find the "fishy" flavor of the caviar is not a good match with the acid of the champagne. A pilsner, on the other hand, has a dry and slightly bitter flavor that matches the "sea" flavor of cavier. In fact, it goes well with anything that is salty or a little oily. A Spaten or dry lager like a Pilsner Urquell would be perfect with caviar or smoked salmon. Put the beer in a flute and enjoy!

Most beer is brewed with a small portion of roasted grain. The more roasted malt that is used in a beer the better it goes with grilled foods. Chef Moonen explained:

One of my favorite ways to prepare foods is to grill them. Here is a good chance to enjoy a dark beer. Many of them [dark beers] have a slight smoky flavor from the roasted grains used in the brewing process. These work great with grilled foods. One of the combinations I have used is a stout with cherry-grilled filet mignon. The lean beef and the cherry wood smoke went great with the rich and slightly smokey flavor of the stout.

MAIBOCK AT THE WALDORF-ASTORIA

Chef John Doherty of the Waldorf Astoria has been executive chef at the landmark hotel since 1985. A graduate of the Culinary Institute of America, Chef Doherty has been a guest chef at the Hotel Ritz in Paris; the Grand Hotel in Stockholm; the Greenbriar in White Sulphur Springs, West Virginia; and Chez Melange in Los Angeles.

In the summer of 1993, Jim Munson, from the Brooklyn Brewery, approached the beverage director of the Waldorf-Astoria in New York with a selection of beers he was marketing. The beverage director and Munson went to Chef Doherty and asked whether he would be interested in developing menu items to go with the beers.

Chef Doherty was intrigued. He told Munson, "I like good beer as much as anyone else; leave me some samples and I'll check it out." As a result, over two afternoons, Chef Doherty and Jim Munson tasted, and compared, over 60 beers. While exploring all those beers, Chef Doherty remembered,

I began to get very excited because I didn't know they were so diversified or complex. As I tasted the beers I started thinking of all the foods I make and how the the taste flavors would complement the flavors of each beer. From there we just started writing menus.

In the autumn of 1993 the Waldorf-Astoria's Bull & Bear restaurant began a series of "beer menus," matching seasonal beers with seasonal dishes, which they have continued ever since.

When I asked Chef Doherty whether there were any particularly challenging combinations he could think of, he recalled that in the spring of 1994, he had to match a classic maibock with a springtime menu.

The maibocks were pretty heavy, rich beers and, normally, when we think about food in the springtime we think about light dishes. That was a little challenging but you can still have light food with bold flavor. We did a crisp, roast duck, on a bed of marinated Washington State cherries and braised savoy cabbage. We served that dish with Stouds Honey Double Maibock. The duck, Washington cherries, and cabbage balanced the maibock perfectly.

When I asked how the idea of presenting a "beer menu" has gone over with Waldorf guests, Chef Doherty was quick to answer. "I think it has been received very well. It's been a real education for me. "

THE CHEF'S BEER

Michel Notredame, chef/owner of Brigid's, a Belgian restaurant, in Philadelphia, Pennsylvania, is no stranger to fine food. With a background in French and European kitchens, he enjoys exchanging unique Belgian beers for the wines traditionally used in many French dishes. When I asked Chef Notredame to describe the difference between Belgian and French cuisine, other than the more liberal acceptance of beer in the Belgian kitchen, he answered, "The biggest difference is that Belgian portions are big enough to feed a German."

In the beginning his menu was mainly an eclectic combination of French, Spanish, and Portuguese dishes, and his beer list was limited to a few well-known brews and an import or two. But then he found a distributor who could supply him with beers from his native Belgium, and his menu took on a new flavor.

What's on his menu now?

Now I have beef Chimey, like beef borguignonne but with the Chimey Rouge instead of red wine. I also prepare a salmon sauté with a mustard and cream sauce that uses Duvel instead of white wine. The Duvel makes it less sweet and gives the reduction a nice tart taste that goes perfectly with the mustard and caper.

When the owners of Stoudt's Brewing Company asked Chef Michel Notredame why he didn't have a Belgian beer on draft, to go with his Belgian-inspired dishes, he challenged them, "Brew me an authentic Belgian beer and I will carry it." Together they went to Belgium and sampled hundreds of beers. When the Stoudts returned they were as good as their word. As you can see, now Chef Notredame has his own beer.

Chef Michel Notredame's Belgian-Style Beer

COOKING WITH WORT

Chef Billy Hahn of the Harbor Side, in Portland, Oregon, has been a chef for 21 years. He started out in the Midwest, in Chicago and Michigan. For 13 years he worked with the McCormick organization and then found his way to Portland, where he soon found himself working at the Harbor Side, right next door to the Full Sail micro-brewery. Chef Hahn began using beer from next door in many of his dishes but soon made a startling discovery.

What I found was that what works best is to use the wort from next door; the beer before it is fermented. It has a rich, almost caramel flavor that makes a nice rich reduction for sauces. The sauces we make with organic fruit and various stocks are even better when made with wort. An apricot sauce based on a fish stock, made with a wort reduction, with a little ginger and thickened with a touch of cornstarch, is perfect with a sautéed or baked salmon.

For those of use who don't live next-door to a brewery, Chef Hahn suggests a visit to a local home-brew shop.

From what I understand, people are able to get reduced wort in the home-brewing stores in the form of canned "malt extract." There are a wide range of these extracts, from light to very dark (stout). Just remember to get the unhopped extract. The hopped version just doesn't work.

Finally, I asked Chef Hahn if he ever used the finished beers from next-door. His enthusiasm was hard to conceal.

Full Sails' finished beer works really well as a steaming mixture, especially when we do a traditional clam bake with mussels and clams. We use a little bit of fresh ginger in the beer to help to cut the bitterness a little bit.

SOUPS, STEWS, AND SMOKING

Chef Benito Malivert began his career in France and has spent the last 20 years in the San Francisco Bay area. In 1993 he took over as chef at the Pacific Tap & Grill, a pub-brewery in San Rafael, California.

Trained in kitchens that used wine almost exclusively in recipes, he was fascinated by the flavors of the different beers that were brewed at Pacific Tap & Grill. He is not alone in pointing out that a beer reduction can become very bitter, but he is an enthusiastic proponent of using beer in dishes that are enhanced by combining beer with stock.

Last month I used a porter-style beer with onions and peppers to make a broth to go with a dish of mussels, but my favorite way to use beer in the kitchen is to use it in soups and stews. We have used a porter in a chili that added just the right flavor and texture. I'm looking forward to using our amber beer soon as a marinade for my smoked baby back ribs.

BEER WITH A SWEET TOOTH

Marc Kadish, owner of the Sunset Grill & Tap and the Boston Beer Works, in Boston, Massachusetts boasts that his Sunset Grill & Tap has the most beer taps of any restaurant on the East Coast. He tries to never step over the line in his enthusiasm for beer and food combinations, especially in the kitchen.

Although beer is a perfect ingredient in full-flavored dishes, he says, "We have used Sam Adams triple in a chicken dish. The triple was really sweet, and the bitter flavors were matched with lime and cilantro."

Kadish points out that although it is a real temptation to try to put beer in everything just to say that it's in there, you have to remember that sometimes beer goes better with some foods when it is used as an accompaniment, rather than an ingredient.

"We use beer sparingly in our kitchens. We want beer to complement the food so my staff suggests that people enjoy the flavor combinations that happen when beer is used as the beverage of choice with a meal."

When it comes to desserts though, Kadish goes the full nine yards. His menu features a Guinness ice cream (he makes a reduction of Guinness and chocolate in his kitchen and takes it to a local ice cream shop where the frozen treat is made).

And then, there is the Guinness "Float." Kadish told me, "At Sunset we do what we call a Guinness Float, a large glass of Guinness with the Guinness ice cream on top." Does it raise a few eyebrows? "Sure, but it tastes great!"

RECIPES

After reading about all the interesting ways the previous chefs have to use beer in the kitchen, I am sure some of you would like to try a recipe or two. No special techniques are needed, just a basic understanding of cooking and an appreciation of good food. The next four pages give instructions for creating an appetizer, a soup, a Belgian-style main dish, and a surprising dessert.

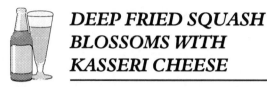

DEEP FRIED SQUASH BLOSSOMS WITH KASSERI CHEESE

(Yields 8–10 blossoms, or one or two appetizers.)

2⅔–3 cups all-purpose flour
1 T salt
¾ tsp. freshly ground pepper
2 T melted butter
4 large eggs, separated; yolks
    beaten lightly, whites
    reserved

12 oz. amber beer
⅔ –1 cup cold water
8–10 squash blossoms
Kasseri cheese, freshly grated
½ cup fresh tomato sauce
Peanut oil for deep frying
Fresh oregano for garnish

1. Combine the flour, salt, and pepper. Drizzle the butter and beaten egg yolks over the dry ingredients while stirring to incorporate. Gradually add the beer and ⅓ cup cold water. Beat until smooth if a long resting time is allowed. (For a more tempura-like batter, do not beat well; mix only enough to incorporate the beer and water without attempting to eliminate the lumps.)
2. Cover and refrigerate the batter, allowing it to rest for at least three hours or overnight.
3. Adjust the consistency of the batter by adding ⅓ –⅔ cups of cold water, or none if a thick batter is desired.
4. Beat the reserved egg whites to stiff peaks and fold into batter.
5. Lightly pack the blossoms of any variety of baby squash with grated Kasseri cheese, and twist the ends to close up securely. Dip the squash blossoms in the batter and deep fry in peanut oil at 375°F until light gold in color. Drain.
6. Serve on a round plate on a circle of fresh tomato sauce. Garnish with sprigs of fresh oregano

(Chef Nancy Schwartz—Stoyanof's, Corte Madera, California)

CHEDDAR BEER SOUP

(Yields 4 servings.)

2 cups cooked carrots, chopped fine	2 T garlic, pressed
1 medium sweet onion, finely chopped	2 T dried parsley, crushed
	12 oz. beer
1 cup butter	2 cups half and half
1 cup flour	1 lb. cheddar cheese, grated
2 cups chicken stock	Salt and pepper to taste
	Popcorn for garnish

1. Sauté the onion in butter until soft. Add flour and whisk together to make a roux. Cook over low heat for three to five minutes but do not brown.
2. Add chicken stock, 1 cup at a time, and garlic and parsley while continuing to whisk. Add beer and continue to stir. Add half and half and carrots. Stir until well blended.
3. Heat soup through over low heat. Serve with popcorn garnish.

(Chef Nancy Kinney—The Brown Bottle, Milwaukee, Wisconsin)

RABBIT IN
KRIEK BEER SAUCE

(Yields 2 servings.)

1 rabbit
3 T butter, divided
2 T flour
1 cup veal stock

⅓ bottle Kriek beer
Salt and pepper to taste
Fresh pitted cherries for garnish

1. Preheat oven to 350°F. Cut rabbit into serving pieces. Pat dry and rub with salt and pepper. Sauté in 2 T butter until golden brown and place in the oven for 30 minutes. Remove from oven and set rabbit aside, keep warm. Reserve the pan and accumulated juices.
2. Dust the pan with flour. Deglaze with beer. Add 3 oz. veal stock and cook to reduce by half. Add salt and pepper to taste and whisk in remaining 1 T butter for a shiny finish to the sauce.
3. Place rabbit pieces on a warm plate; nappe with sauce, and garnish with cherries. Serve with steamed carrots and potatoes.

(Chef Raymond Amaye—Flamand, Manhattan, New York)

 ## *NAUGHTY GRETCHEN*

(Yields 1 serving.)

2 scoops chocolate ice cream
1 12-oz bottle of dark
 or amber beer
One cherry

Place the ice cream in a blender. Add the beer to the ice cream and blend until frothy. Pour into a tall glass and place the cherry on top.

(Jim Gagnier—The Broome Street Bar, Manhattan, New York)

APPENDIX 1
Breweries of the United States and Canada

This is a list of breweries, by state and province. I have tried to find a "pub-brewery" and a "commercial" brewery to represent each state and province. If you discover that any listed here have gone out of business, please let me know. If there is a new brewery or brew pub you would like to have listed in a future edition of this book, also let me know. Keep in mind that the industry is volatile, to say the least, so call ahead before you visit to make sure the brewery or pub-brewery is still in operation.

There is no attempt to rate the quality of the products brewed by these establishments; only the fact that they exist is offered for your edification. I have included this section so that you can find some examples of fresh beer near where you live. Getting to know what fresh beer tastes like is invaluable to understanding beer in general, and to appreciating good beer specifically.

ALABAMA

Birmingham
BIRMINGHAM BREWING CO.
3118 3rd Avenue S.
Birmingham, AL 35233
(205) 326-6677

ALASKA

Anchorage
BIRD CREEK BREWERY
310 East 76th Street (Unit B)
Anchorage, AK 99518
(907) 344-2473

Juneau
ALASKAN BREWING CO.
5429 Shanne Drive
Juneau, AK 99801
(907) 780-5866

ARIZONA

Phoenix
COYOTE SPRINGS
BREWING CO.
4883 N. 20th Street
Phoenix, AZ 85016
(602) 468-0403

Scottsdale
HOPS BISTRO AND
BREWERY (pub-brewery)
7000 East Camelback Road, #110
Scottsdale, AZ 85251
(602) 945-4677

Tempe
BANDERSHACHBREWPUB
125 East 5th Avenue
Tempe, AZ 85281
(602) 966-4438

Tuscon
GENTLE BEN'S BREWING CO.
841 N. Tyndall
Tuscon, AZ 85719
(602) 624-4177

ARKANSAS

Fayetteville
OZARK BREWING CO.
430 W. Dickenson Street
Fayetteville, AR 72701
(501) 521-2739

Fort Smith
WEIDMANS BREW PUB
4222 North Third
Fort Smith, AR 72901
(501) 782-9898

Little Rock
VINO'S (pub-brewery)
923 West Seventh
Little Rock, AR 72201
(501) 375-8466

CALIFORNIA

Arcata
HUMBOLT BREWING CO.
856 10th Street
Arcata, CA 95521
(707) 826-2739

Berkeley
BISON BREWING CO.
  (brew pub)
2598 Telegraph Avenue
Berkeley, CA 94704
(510) 841-7734

Boonville
ANDERSON VALLEY
BREWING CO.
14081 Highway 128
Boonville, CA 95415
(707) 895-2337

Chico
SIERRA NEVADA
BREWING CO.
1075 East 20th Street
Chico, CA 95928
(916) 345-2739

Hayward
BUFFALO BILL'S BREWERY
(brew pub)
1082 B Street
Hayward, CA 94541
(510) 886-9823

Hopland
MENDOCINO BREWING
CO. (brew pub)
13351 South Highway 101
Hopland, CA 95449
(707) 744-1015

Modesto
ST. STAN'S BREWING CO.
821 L Street
Modesto, CA 95354
(209) 524-2337

San Francisco
ANCHOR BREWING CO.
1705 Mariposa Street
San Francisco, CA 94107
(415) 863-8350

COLORADO
Denver
WYNKOOP BREWING CO.
1634 18th Street
Denver, CO 80202
(303) 297-2700

Golden
COORS BREWING CO.
12th and Ford
Golden, CO 80401
(303) 279-6565

CONNECTICUT
New Haven
NEW HAVEN BREWING CO.
458 Grand Avenue
New Haven, CT 06513
(203) 772-2739

Norwalk
NEW ENGLAND
BREWING CO.
13 Marshall Street
Norwalk, CT 06854
(203) 866-1339

DELAWARE
Newark
BLUE HEN BEER CO.
(302) 737-8375
Brewed by The Lion,
Wilkes-Barre, PA

DISTRICT OF COLUMBIA
THE OLD HEURICH
BREWING CO.
1111 34th Street NW
Washington, DC 20007
(202) 333-2313
Brewed by F.X. Matt Co, Utica, NY

FLORIDA

Tampa
HOPS GRILL & BAR INC.
(pub brewery)
3030 N. Rocky Point Drive West
Tampa, FL 33607
(813) 282-9350
also in: Clearwater, Palm Harbor,
Lakeland, and Jacksonville, FL.

Fort Myers
THE MILL BAKERY, EATERY
& BREWERY(pub-brewery)
11491 Cleveland Avenue
Fort Myers, FL 33907
(813) 939-2739
also in: Tallahassee, Gainsville,
and Winter Park, FL, and
Charlotte, NC

GEORGIA

Atlanta
FRIENDS BREWING CO.
Atlanta, GA 30359
(404) 986-8505

ATLANTA BREWING CO.
Atlanta, GA
(404) 892-4436

IDAHO

Boise
TABLE ROCK BREWPUB &
GRILL (pub-brewery)
705 West Fulton
Boise, ID 83702
(208) 342-0944

Hailey
THE SUN VALLEY BREWING
CO. (pub-brewery)

202 North Main
Hailey, ID 83333
(208) 788-5777

ILLINOIS

Chicago
GOOSE ISLAND BREWING
CO. (pub-brewery)
1800 North Clybourn
Chicago, IL 60614
(312) 915-0071

Elmhurst
PAVICHEVICH BREWING CO.
38 Romans Road
Elmhurst, IL 60126
(708) 617-5252

INDIANA

Indianapolis
BROAD RIPPLE BREWING
CO. (pub-brewery)
840 East 65th Street
Indianapolis, IN 46220
(317) 253-2739

INDIANAPOLIS BREWING CO.
3250 North Post Road
Indianapolis, IN 46226

IOWA

Amana
MILLSTREAM BREWING CO.
Amana, IA 52203
(319) 622-3672

Davenport
FRONT STREET BREWERY
(pub-brewery)
208 E. River Drive
Davenport, IA 52801
(319) 322-1569

Dubuque
DUBUQUE BREWING CO.
500 East Fourth Street
Dubuque, IA 52001-2398

KANSAS

Lawrence
FREE STATE BREWING CO.
636 Massachusetts Street
Lawrence, KS 66044
(913) 843-4555

Wichita
RIVER CITY BREWING CO.
(pub-brewery)
150 N. Mosley
Wichita, KS 67202
(316) 263-2739

KENTUCKY

Fort Mitchell
OLDENBERG BREWING CO.
(pub-brewery)
I-75 at Buttermilk Pike
Fort Mitchell, KY 41017
(606) 341-0411

Louisville
THE SILO BREW PUB
630 Barret Avenue
Louisville, KY 40204
(502) 589-2739

LOUISIANA

Abita Springs
ABITA BREWING CO., INC.
Abita Springs, LA 70420
(504) 893-3143

New Orleans
CRESCENT CITY
BREWHOUSE (pub-brewery)
527 Decatur Street
New Orleans, LA 70130
(504) 522-0571

DIXIE BREWING CO., INC.
2537 Tulane Avenue
New Orleans, LA 70119
(504) 822-8711

MAINE

Portland
D.L. GEARY BREWING CO.,
INC.
38 Evergreen Drive
Portland, ME 04103
(207) 878-2337

GRITTY McDUFF'S BREW PUB
396 Fore Street
Portland, ME 04101
(207) 772-2739

MARYLAND

Baltimore
BALTIMORE BREWING CO.
(pub-brewery)
104 Albermarle Street
Baltimore, MD 21202
(410) 837-5000

SISSON'S SOUTH
BALTIMORE BREWING CO.
(pub-brewery)
36 East Cross Street
Baltimore, MD 21201
(410) 244-8900

Cambridge
WILD GOOSE BREWERY
20 Washington Street
Cambridge, MD 21613
(410) 221-1121

Gaithersburg
OLDE TOWNE TAVERN &
  BREWERY CO. (pub-brewery)
227 E. Diamond Avenue
Gaithersburg, MD 20877
(301) 948-4200

MASSACHUSETTS

Boston
BOSTON BEER CO.
  (brewery and brew pub)
30 Germania Street
Boston, MA 02130
(617) 522-3400

COMMONWEALTH
  BREWING CO. (pub-brewery)
138 Portland Street
Boston, MA 02114
(617) 523-8383

MASS BAY BREWING CO.
306 Northern Avenue
Boston, MA 02210
(617) 951-4099

MICHIGAN

Detroit
DETROIT & MACKINAC
  BREWERY, LTD.
407 West Canfield
Detroit, MI 48201
(313) 831-2739

Frankenmuth
FRANKENMUTH BREWERY
INC.
425 South Main Street
Frankenmuth, MI 48734
(517) 652-6183

MINNESOTA

Cold Spring
COLD SPRING BREWING
  CO., INC.
219 North Red River Avenue
Cold Spring, MN 56320
(612) 685-8686

New Ulm
AUGUST SCHELL BREWING
  CO., INC.
Schell's Park
New Ulm, MN 56073
(507) 354-5528

St. Paul
MINNESOTA BREWING CO.
882 West 7th Street
St. Paul, MN 55102
(612) 228-9173

SUMMIT BREWING CO.
2264 University Avenue
St. Paul, MN 55114
(612) 645-5029

MISSISSIPPI

Eupora
KERSHENSTEIN DIAMOND
(brewed by Dixie Brewing Co.)
401 Industrial Park (Dept AAB)
Eupora, MS 39744
(601) 258-2049

MISSOURI

Kansas City
BOULEVARD BREWING CO.
2501 Southwest Boulevard
Kansas City, MO 64108
(816) 474-7095

St. Louis
ANHEUSER-BUSCH, INC.
One Busch Plaza
St. Louis, MO 63118-1852
(314) 577-2000

MONTANA

Helena
KESSLER BREWING CO.
1439 Harris Street
Helena, MT 59601
(406) 449-6214

Missoula
BAYERN BREWING, INC.
Missoula, MT 59807-8043
(406) 594-6444

NEBRASKA

Lincoln
CRANE RIVER BREWPUB &
CAFE
200 North 11th Street
Lincoln, NE 68508
(402) 476-7766

Omaha
JONES STREET BREWERY
1316 Jones Street
Omaha, NE 68102
(402) 344-3858

NEVADA

Las Vegas
HOLY COW! BREWING CO.
2423 Las Vegas Boulevard
Las Vegas, NV 89104
(702) 732-2697

Virginia City
UNION BREWERY BEER
(pub-brewery)
28 North C Street
Virginia City, NV 89440
(702) 847-0328

NEW HAMPSHIRE

Nashua
MARTHA'S EXCHANGE
BREWING CO.
185 Main Street
Nashua, NH 03060
(603) 883-8781

Portsmouth
PORTSMOUTH BREWERY
56 Market Street
Portsmouth, NH 03801
(603) 431-1115

NEW JERSEY

Brigantine
ATLANTIC CITY BREWING
CO.
(brewed by The Lion, PA)
Brigantine, NJ 08203
(609) 641-7884

Vernon
CLEMENT'S BREWING CO.
Route 94 Cobblestone Village
Vernon, NJ 07462
(201) 827-0344

NEW MEXICO

Albuquerque
ASSETS GRILLE & BREWING
CO. (pub-brewery)
6910 Montgomery N.E.
Albuquerque, NM 87110
(505) 889-6400

Galisteo
THE SANTA FE BREWING CO.
Flying M Ranch
Galisteo, NM 87540
(505) 988-2340

NEW YORK

Albany
WM. S. NEWMAN BREWING
CO., INC.
(brewed by Catamount, VT)
84 Chestnut Street
Albany, NY 12210
(518) 465-8501

Ithaca
CHAPTER HOUSE BREWPUB
400 Stewart Avenue
Ithaca, NY 14850
(607) 277-4146

New York
THE MANHATTAN
BREWING CO.
42 Thompson Street
New York, NY 10013
(212) 925-1515

ZIP CITY BREWING CO.
3 West 18th Street
New York, NY 10011
(212) 366-6333

Utica
F.X. MATT BREWING CO.
811 Edward Street
Utica, NY 13502
(315) 732-3181

NORTH CAROLINA

Charlotte
DILWORTH BREWING CO.
1301 East Boulevard
Charlotte, NC 28203
(704) 377-2739

Manteo
WEEPING RADISH BAVARIAN
RESTAURANT & BREWERY
Highway 64
Manteo, NC 27954
(919) 473-1157

NORTH DAKOTA

Grand Forks
DAKOTA BREWING CO.
(brewed by Minnesota Brewing
Co., MN)
Grand Forks, ND 58206
(701) 775-0187

OHIO

Columbus
THE GAMBRINUS
BREWING CO.
1152 South Front Street
Columbus, OH 43206
(614) 444-7769

HOSTER BREWING CO.
(pub-brewery)
550 South High Street
Columbus, OH 43215
(614) 228-6066

OKLAHOMA

Oklahoma City
BRICKTOWN BREWERY
(pub-brewery)
1 North Oklahoma Avenue
Oklahoma City, OK 73104
(405) 232-2739

Tulsa
CHERRY STREET BREWERY
(pub-brewery)
1516 South Quaker
Tulsa, OK 74152
(918) 582-2739

OREGON

Ashland
ROGUE BREWERY &
PUBLIC HOUSE
31-B Water Street
Ashland, OR 97520
(503) 488-5061

Beaverton
McMENAMIN'S (pub-brewery)
6179 S.W. Murray Boulevard
Beaverton, OR 97005
(503) 644-4562

Hood River
FULL SAIL BREWING CO.
506 Columbia
Hood River, OR 97031
(503) 386-2281

Portland
PORTLAND BREWING CO.
2730 N.W. 31st Street
Portland, OR 97201
(503) 222-7150

WIDMER BREWING CO.
929 N. Russell
Portland, OR 97227
(503) 281-2437

PENNSYLVANIA

Adamstown
STOUDT BREWING CO.
Route 272
Adamstown, PA 19501
(215) 484-4387

Latrobe
LATROBE BREWING CO.
119 Jefferson Street
Latrobe, PA 15650
(412) 537-5545

Philadelphia
DOCK STREET BREWING
CO.
Two Logan Square
18th & Cherry Streets
Philedelphia, PA 19103
(215) 496-0413

Pottsville
D.G. YUENGLING & SONS,
INC.
5th & Manhantongo Streets
Pottsville, PA 17901
(717) 622-4141

SOUTH DAKOTA

Rapid City
FIREHOUSE BREWING CO.
610 Main Street
Rapid City, SD 57701
(605) 348-1915

TENNESSEE

Germantown
BOSCOS PIZZA KITCHEN &
BREWERY
7615 West Farmington
Germantown, TN 38138
(901) 756-7310

Nashville
BOHANNON BREWING CO.
134 Second Avenue North
Nashville, TN 37201
(615) 242-8223

TEXAS

Austin
CELIS BREWERY INC.
2431 Forbes Drive
Austin, TX 78714
(512) 835-0844

Shiner
SPOETZL BREWERY
Shiner, TX 77984
(512) 594-3852

UTAH

Moab
EDDIE McSTIFF'S BREWPUB
57 South Main
Moab, UT 84532
(801) 259-2337

Salt Lake City
SQUATTERS PUB BREWERY
147 West Broadway
Salt Lake City, UT 84101
(801) 363-2739

VERMONT

Burlington
THE VERMONT PUB &
BREWERY OF BURLINGTON
144 College Street
Burlington, VT 05401
(802) 865-0500

White River Junction
THE CATAMOUNT
BREWING CO.
58 Main Street
White River Junction, VT 05001
(802) 296-2248

VIRGINIA

Ashburn
OLD DOMINION BREWING
CO.
4633 Guilford Drive
Ashburn, VA 22011
(703) 689-1225

Charlottesville
BLUE RIDGE BREWING CO.
709 West Main
Charlottesville, VA 22901
(804) 977-0017

WASHINGTON

Kalama
HART BREWING
CO./PYRAMID ALES
110 West Marine Drive
Kalama, WA 98625
(206) 673-2121

Kirkland
HALE'S ALES LTD.
109 Central Way
Kirkland, WA 98033
(206) 827-4359

Seattle
THE REDHOOK ALE
BREWERY
3400 Phinney Avenue N.
Seattle, WA 98103
(206) 548-8000

Yakima
YAKIMA BREWING &
MALTING CO., INC.
1803 Presson Place
Yakima, WA 98903
(509) 575-1900

WEST VIRGINIA

Morgantown
WEST VIRGINIA BREWING
CO. (pub-brewery)
1291 University Avenue
Morgantown, WV 26505
(304) 296-2739

WISCONSIN

Milwaukee
SPRECHER BREWING CO.,
INC.
730 West Oregon Street
Milwaukee, WI 53204
(414) 272-2739

Stevens Point
STEVENS POINT BREWERY
2617 Water Street
Stevens Point, WI 54481
(715) 344-9310

WYOMING

Jackson
OTTO BROTHERS
BREWING CO.
Jackson, WY 83001
(307) 733-9000

CANADIAN BREWERIES

ALBERTA

Calgary
BIG ROCK BREWERY LTD.
6403 35th Street
Calgary, Alberta T2C 1N2
(403) 279-2917

BREWSTERS BREW PUB &
BRASSERIE
834-11th Avenue, S.W.
Calgary, Alberta T2R 0E5
(403) 263-2739

BRITISH COLUMBIA

Horseshoe Bay
HORSESHOE BAY BREWERY
6695 Nelson Avenue
Horseshoe Bay, British
Columbia V7W 2B2

Nelson
THE NELSON BREWING
CO., LTD
512 Latimer Stret
Nelson, British Columbia
V1L 4T9
(604) 352-3582

Vancouver
GRANVILLE ISLAND
BREWING, LTD.
1441 Cartwright Street
Vancouver, British Columbia
V6H 3R7
(604) 688-9927

Victoria
SPINNAKERS BREW PUB INC.
308 Catherine Street
Victoria, British Columbia
V0S 1M0
(604) 384-0332

MANITOBA
Both Labatt and Molson have
breweries in this province.

NEW BRUNSWICK
Saint John
MOOSEHEAD BREWERIES
LTD.
89 Main Street
P.O. Box 3100, Station B
Saint John, New Brunswick
E2M 3H2
(506) 635-7000

NEWFOUNDLAND
Both Labatt and Molson have
breweries in this province.

NOVA SCOTIA
Halifax
THE GRANITE BREWERY
Henry House
1222 Barrington Street
Halifax, Nova Scotia B3J 1Y2
(902) 422-4954

ONTARIO
ALGONQUIN BREWING
COMPANY
Number One Brewery Lane
Formosa, Ontario
(519) 367-2995

CREEMORE SPRINGS
139 Mill Street
Creemore, Ontario
(705) 466-2531

BRICK BREWING
181 King Street
Waterloo, Ontario
(519) 576-9100

CONNOR'S BREWERY
227 Bunting Road, Unit J
St. Catherines, Ontario
(905) 988-9363

GREAT LAKES BREWING
30 Queen Elizabeth Boulevard
Etobicoke, Ontario
(416) 255-4510

HART BREWERIES LTD.
175 Industrial Avenue
Carleton Place, Ontario
(613) 253-4278

NIAGARA FALLS BREWING
COMPANY
6863 Lundy's Lane
Niagara Falls, Ontario
(905) 356-BREW

SLEEMAN'S BREWING AND
MALTING
551 Claire Road West
Guelph, Ontario
(519) 822-1834

UPPER CANADA BREWING
   COMPANY
2 Atlantic Avenue
Toronto, Ontario
(416) 534- 9281

WELLINGTON COUNTY
   BREWERY
950 Woodlawn Road
Guelph, Ontario
(519) 837-2337

QUEBEC

La Salle
BRASSERIE BRASAL
   BREWERY INC.
8477 rue Cordner
LaSalle, Quebec H8N 2X2
(514) 365-5050

Lennoxville
GOLDEN LION BREWING CO.
6 College Street
Lennoxville, Quebec J1M 1Z6
(819) 562-4589

Montreal
BAR LE CERVOISE
4457 St. Lawrence Boulevard
Montreal, Quebec H2W 1Z8

LE BRASSEURS G.M.T. INC
5710 rue Garnier
Montreal, Quebec H2G 2Z7

LE CHEVAL BLANC
805 Ontario East
Montreal, Quebec H2L 1P1
(514) 522-0211

CROCODILE GATINEAU
5412-4 Gatineau Street

Montreal, Quebec H3T 1X5
(514) 733- 2125

CROCODILE ST. LAURENT
4236-8 rue St. Laurent
Montreal, Quebec H2W 1Z3

McAUSLAN BREWING INC.
4850 Ambroise Street
Montreal, Quebec H4C 3N8
(514) 939-3060

St. Jerome
LES BRASSEURS DU NORD
   INC.
18 Boulivard J. F. Kennedy
St. Jerome, Quebec J7Y 4B4
(514) 438-9060

St. Lazare
MON VILLAGE BREWERY
2760 Cote Street/Charles Road
St. Lazare, Quebec J0P 1V0

SASKATCHEWAN

Regina
BARLEY MILL BREWING
   COMPANY
6807 Rochdale Boulevard N.W.
Regina, Saskatchewan S4X 2Z2
(306) 949-1500

BONZINI'S BREWPUB
4634 Albert Street
Regina, Saskatchewan S4S 6B4

BREWSTERS BREWPUB AND
   BRASSERIE
1832 Victoria Avenue E.
Regina, Saskatchewan S4N 7K3
(306) 761-1500

BUSHWAKKER BREWING
CO. LTD.
2206 Dewdney Avenue
Regina, Saskatchewan S4R 1H3
(306) 359-7276

LUXEMBOURG BREWPUB
127 Albert Street N.
Regina, Saskatchewan S4R 8C7
(306) 545-1911

Saskatoon
CHEER'S BREW PUB
32-2105 8th Street E.
Saskatoon, Saskatchewan S7K 5M8
(306) 955-7500

CLARK'S CROSSING
BREWPUB
3030 Diefenbaker
Saskatoon, Saskatchewan S7L 7K2
(306) 384-6633

FOX & HOUND BREWPUB
117 Assiniboine Drive
Saskatoon, Saskatchewan S7K 4C1
(306) 664-2233

GREAT WESTERN BREWING
COMPANY LTD.
519 Second Avenue N.
Saskatoon, Saskatchewan S7K 2C6

APPENDIX 2
WEiqHTS ANd MEASURES

I. Larger Measures of Capacity

Barrel: For beer, usually 31 gallons, for wine 31.5 gallons.

Firkin: For wine, 84 gallons; for ale or beer, ¼ barrel or 9 gallons. (This is no mistake; the two firkins are indeed vastly different in size.)

Gallon: For ale, 282 cu in; for wine 231 cu in. Note that the 231-cu-in wine gallon is identical to the U.S. gallon. This was the legal size of the gallon as established under Queen Anne in 1707. Also, the 282-cu-in ale gallon is 1.65% larger than the 277.42-cu-in Imperial gallon!

Kilderkin: 18 gallons.

Pin: 4.5 gallons.

Quart:
Ale Quart:	70.50 cu in
Imperial Quart:	69.36 cu in
Reputed Quart:	46.24 cu in
	(i.e., ⅔ of the Imperial Quart)
	(Also known as the Whiskey Quart)
Wine Quart:	57.75 cu in
	(i.e., the same as the U.S. Quart)

Quarter: 64 gallons, ¼ of a tun.

Tun: A measure of capacity for wine and ale, originally 256 gallons. For wine, the tun lost 4 gallons and dropped to 252 gallons.

Pottle: This term was used for ½ gallon in reference to beer.

II. Drinking Vessels and Bottles

Thurdendel: A drinking vessel used in the seventeenth century for malt liquors, somewhat larger than the requisite capacity so that a full measure of liquid may be obtained with the froth on top, similar in intent to the modern "line" beer glass.

Pounder: A colloquial expression used in reference to a 16-fl-oz can of beer.

Yard: A drinking vessel measuring 36 inches from its base to its lip, featuring a large round base and a long tapered neck that flares quite widely at the top. This glass was originally used to provide coachmen their ale at stops, allowing the server to pass the vessel to the coachman without the coachman having to get down off the coach. The capacity varies, but 2.5 pints and 4.5 pints are the most common sizes.

Today the yard is a novelty that can be found in a number of fine pubs. In many cases, it is used in drinking contests, particulary those involving timed consumption. The *Guinness Book of Records* last reported records for such a contest in 1990. There are also Half-Yard and Foot glasses of the same style.

Line Glass: A glass with the rated capacity shown as a line near the top of the glass.

III. Small Measures: U.S., U.K., and Metric Equivalents

Name	System/Abbrev.	ounces	cc/ml
gallon	US gal	128	3785.413
quart	US qt	32	946.353
pint	US pt	16	473.177
gill	US gi	4	118.294
fluid ounce	US fl oz	1	29.574
fluid dram	US fl dr	1/8	3.69669
gallon	UK gal	160	4546
quart	UK qt	40	1136
pint	UK pt	20	568.26
gill	UK gi	5	142.066
fluid ounce	UK fl oz	1	28.412
fluid dram	UK fl dr	1/8	3.5516

APPENDIX 3
Alcohol Content

When Prohibition was repealed, the power to regulate alcohol was granted to the individual states. Thus, the rules regarding alcohol content vary greatly from one state to another. The only exception to this rule is the federal regulation on container labeling. In the United States you can label any fermented malt beverage as "Beer" as long as it is less than 5% alcohol by volume (abv). Anything over 5% alcohol by volume must be labeled as "Malt Liquor." *Regular beer* and *malt liquor* are not brewing terms but as far as the federal government is concerned, if you brew a lager that is 5% alcohol, it is a beer; if it is 5.1% alcohol, it is a malt liquor.

A "typical" beer contains between 4.5% and 5% alcohol by volume (or about 3.5%–4% alcohol by weight). The norm for the U.S. mega-brewery products (about 4% by weight) is the same as for Canadian mega-brewery products (about 5% by volume). For some reason, people don't seem to believe it, though. It's a frequent mistake made by those "documenting" that Canadian beers are stronger than American beers. (Just for the record, it is possible to brew beers with alcohol contents ranging from negligible [less than 3% abv] to very potent (Sam Adams Triple Bock at around 17% abv]). As an example, consider how many people are convinced that Canadian (or German or English or [insert country of choice here]) beers are much more alcoholic than American beers.

APPENDIX 4
Beer and Food Chart

Here is a simple chart of beer and food matings that can be used to design menus for home and professional kitchens. Special thanks to Chef Rick Moonen of Oceana for his help.

STYLE OF BEER Suggested Brand	MENU SUGGESTION
AMERICAN LIGHT LAGER Budweiser	Pizza, fried chicken, hot dogs
EUROPEAN PILSNER Pilsner Urquell	Caviar, smoked salmon
BRITISH BITTER Fuller's London Pride	Meat pies
PALE ALE Bass	Fish and chips
INDIA PALE ALE Liberty Ale	Roast game, venison
VIENNA LAGER Dos Equis	Roast pork, chicken
BROWN ALE Newcastle Brown Ale	Beef stew
SCOTTISH ALE McEwan's Scotch Ale	Braised rabbit
STRONG ALE Theakston's Old Peculier	After-dinner drink

STYLE OF BEER Suggested Brand	MENU SUGGESTION
BARLEYWINE Anchor Old Foghorn	Maytag blue cheese and walnuts
BOCK BEER Salvatore	Roast goose
PORTER Yeungling Porter	Boiled beef dinner
STOUT Guinness Stout	Oysters on the half shell
WHEAT BEER Paulaner Hefe-Weizen	Cold cut meats
SMOKED BEER Kaiserdom Rauchbier	Smoked sausages
STRONG LAGER Samichlaus Bier	Chocolate
OKTOBERFEST Paulaner Octoberfest Marzen	Roast chicken

BELGIAN BEERS

Every Belgian beer has a particular Belgian cheese that goes with it. The menu choices listed here are in place of those cheeses, almost none of which are available in the United States or Canada.

Rodenbach	Pickled herring
Lindemans Kriek	Stews (beef/fish)
Lindemans Gueuze	Roasted meats
Liefmans Frambozenbier	Soft cheeses (Brie)
Duvel	Roast meats/game
Chimay	Roast game girds

Bibliography

Baron, Stanley. *Brewed in America: A History of Beer and Ale in the United States.* Boston: Little, Brown & Co., 1962.

Eckhardt, Fred. *The Essentials of Beer Style.* Portland, OR: Fred Eckhardt Associates, 1989.

Fix, George, and Laurie Fix. *Marzen/Oktoberfest/Vienna.* Classic Beer Styles Series, no. 4. Boulder, CO: Brewers Publications, 1991.

Foster, Terry. *Porter.* Classic Beer Styles Series, no. 5. Boulder, CO: Brewers Publications, 1992.

Foster, Terry. *Pale Ale.* Classic Beer Styles Series, no. 1. Boulder, CO: Brewers Publications, 1990.

Guinard, Jean-Xavier. *Lambic.* Classic Beer Styles Series, no. 3. Boulder, CO: Brewers Publications, 1990.

Jackson, Michael. *Michael Jackson's Beer Companion.* Philadelphia: Running Press, 1993.

———. *The Great Beers of Belgium.* Cooperstown, NY: Vanberg & Dewulf, 1991.

———. *The Simon & Schuster Pocket Guide to Beer.* New York: Simon & Schuster, Fireside, 1991.

———. *The New World Guide to Beer.* Philadelphia: Running Press, 1988.

Kroll, Wayne L. *Badger Breweries.* Jefferson, WI: Wayne L. Kroll. 1976.

Miller, David. *Continental Pilsner.* Classic Beer Styles Series, no. 2. Boulder, CO: Brewers Publications, 1990.

Noonan, Gregory J. *Scotch Ale.* Classic Beer Styles Series, no. 8. Boulder, CO: Brewers Publications, 1993.

———. *Brewing Lager Beer.* Boulder, CO: Brewers Publications, 1986.

Rajotte, Pierre. *Belgian Ale.* Classic Beer Styles Series, no. 6. Boulder, CO: Brewers Publications, 1990.

Warner, Eric. *German Wheat Beer.* Classic Beer Styles Series, no. 7. Boulder, CO: Brewers Publications, 1992.

Glossary

ADJUNCT: An ingredient used in the grist, or added to the wort, that is not malted barley. Examples of adjuncts are corn, rice, sugar, wheat, and other cereal grains. Adjuncts are used to alter flavors or are added because of economic reasons. In some cases, such as in Belgian lambic beers, fruit is added to create unique beers such as kriek (cherries), framboise (raspberries), and pech (peach).

AEROBIC: The word used to describe an organism, such as a top-fermenting ale yeast, that needs oxygen to metabolize.

ALCOHOL (ETHANOL—C_2H_5OH) The by-product of fermentation. The result of yeast metabolizing sugar.

ALCOHOL BY VOLUME: A measurement of the alcohol content of a solution in terms of the percentage volume of alcohol per volume of beer.

To calculate the approximate volumetric alcohol content, subtract the final gravity from original gravity and divide the result by 7.5 (margin of error ±15 %).

ALCOHOL BY WEIGHT: A measurement of the alcohol content of a solution in terms of the percentage weight of alcohol per volume of beer. Example: 3.2% alcohol by weight is equal to 3.2 grams of alcohol per 100 centiliters of beer.

The percent-of-alcohol-by-weight figure is approximately 20% lower than the by-volume figure because alcohol weighs less then its equivalent volume of water.

ALE: A beverage made from malted barley, hops, and water, fermented with a top-fermenting (aerobic) yeast, at a relatively high temperature. Adjuncts can be added, as deemed necessary, to meet the color, flavor, and alcohol content requirements to be brewed in a specific "style." (See Chapter 4, "Styles of Beer.")

ALTBIER: A style of beer from the Dusseldorf region of Germany that is fermented using a top fermenting (ale) yeast and cold conditioned. (Contrast STEAM BEER: lager-yeast fermented and conditioned at ale temperatures.)

ANAEROBIC: A word used to describe an organism, such as a bottom-fermenting lager yeast, that is able to metabolize in the absence of oxygen.

ATTENUATION: The degree to which a beer has fermented; the final gravity expressed as a percentage of the original specific gravity.

BARLEY: A cereal grain that is malted for use in the grist that becomes the mash in the process of brewing beers.

BARLEYWINE: A brew with a high original gravity (up to 11% alcohol by volume). Commercially available examples are Anchor Old Foghorn and Sierra Nevada Bigfoot.

BARREL: A standard of measurement equal to 31 U.S. gallons. In Britain, a standard of measurement equal to 36 Imperial gallons (43.2 U.S. gallons).

BEER: A fermented beverage made from grain, hops, water, yeast, and, in some cases, additional adjuncts.

BIERE DE GARDE: A beer from the northern part of France. Originally made by farmers in the region, these beers are a little over 8% alcohol by volume. They have a medium hop flavoring with slight traces of spice (cinnamon, nutmeg) and a touch of apple or pear.

BITTER: A subclassification of traditional pale ale, with less hop content and carbonation than a traditional pale ale. The distinction between bitter and pale ale has become less and less over the years. Today English brewers have difficulty telling where to draw the line.

BOCK: A dark, strong (6% to 7% alcohol content by volume) lager-style beer, first brewed in the city of Einbeck (pronounced INE-bock) in Bavaria, Germany , in the fourteenth and fifteenth centuries. This style was brewed to survive shipment throughout Europe.

BODY: The consistency of the beer. Body is signified as full-bodied, medium-bodied, or light-bodied. The relative descriptions are used when tasting beers, usually in comparison of one beer with another.

BREW KETTLE (also called copper): The vessel in which wort is boiled with the hops after mashing and before chilling and fermentation.

BREW PUB: A brewery/restaurant where the beer brewed on the premises is dispensed directly from bright tanks, for consumption on the premises only.

BRIGHT TANK: The pressurized fermentation vessel where the beer is kept, chilled and under pressure, until drawn off by the person operating the tap in the brew pub. In a traditional brewery it is used to store beer prior to bottling or kegging.

BROWN ALE: The most famous English brown ale is Newcastle Brown Ale. Other ales of the same type are brewed in the northern part of England. They are nutty in flavor, with mild hopping.

CAMRA (CAMpaign for Real Ale): An organization in England that was founded in 1971 to preserve the production of cask-conditioned beers and ales.

CARAMEL: A cooked sugar that is used to add color and alcohol content to beer. It is often used in place of more expensive malted barley.

CARBON DIOXIDE: The gas by-product of yeast metabolism during fermentation when simple sugars are broken down into alcohol and gas. Under pressure, carbon dioxide causes effervescence in beer.

CASK: A container for draft beer that is designed for beer dispensed at atmospheric pressure. "Cask-conditioned" beers are allowed to finish conditioning in the cask and are served by gravity tap, not under pressure.

CREAM ALE: A beer specific to North America, usually a lager-fermented product with a relatively high alcohol and hop content.

CONDITIONING: The process that causes beer to become effervescent.

COPPER: The large (usually copper) vessel where the wort is boiled with the hops before being chilled and piped into the fermentation tanks. Copper is used because it heats evenly and does not chemically react with the beer while it is boiled with the hops.

DEXTRIN: The unfermentable substance made by the enzymes found naturally in barley. Such substances give beer flavor, body, and mouth feel. By controlling the temperature during the mash, the brew master can determine how much dextrin is produced. Lower temperatures tend to develop more dextrin, while higher temperatures convert the starches to more sugar than dextrin. It gives the "mouth feel" to a beer. Without it, beer would taste thin.

DORTMUNDER: Named after the city in Germany where it is brewed, this is a malty, rich, lightly hopped lager beer with a golden color. It is lighter and less aromatic than a pilsner.

DRAFT (DRAUGHT): The process of dispensing beer from a bright tank, cask, or keg, by hand pump, pressure from an air pump, or injected carbon dioxide inserted into the beer container prior to sealing.

DUNKEL: From the German word meaning "dark." This term is used especially in terms of weiss beers. There are many very famous "Dunkel" wheat beers brewed in the German city of Munich.

ENZYMES: Catalysts that are found naturally in the grain of the barley cereal. When heated in a mash, they convert the starches of the malted barley into maltose, a sugar used in solution and fermented to make beer.

ESTERS: Aromatic oils that are the by-products of fermentation. These are especially prevalent in the metabolization of sugars by top-fermenting ale yeasts. Their characteristic "fruity" aromas are the sign of a well-fermented ale. (Aromatics include apple, pear, pineapple, prune, and the aroma of new-mown hay or lawn grass.)

FARO: Faro is a young lambic that is sweetened and sometimes spiced; when bottled, it's usually pasteurized to keep the added sugar from fermenting.

FRAMBOISE: A Belgian lambic in which ripe raspberries have been added to the fermentation. The raspberries add a refreshing flavor to the rather dry and slightly sour beer.

GRAVITY (specific gravity): The amount of materials (usually sugars) in ratio to a specific measure of water expressed as a percentage. If a specific solution of water and maltose consists of equal parts of sugar and water, the specific gravity is said to be 1.050 or, in brewer's terms, 50 SG. More traditionally, commercial brewers use the terms *balling, or plato* and measure the weight of sugar in solution as a percentage of the weight of the solution (grams per 100 grams of solution).

GRIST: The crushed grains used to make a mash. The grist can consist of any number of grains (barely malt, corn, rice, oatmeal) except in Bavaria, where the Rheinheitsgebot, or Purity Law, decrees that only malted barley can be used.

GUEUZE: A blend of young and old lambic beers are bottled and allowed to continue fermentation in the bottle. The result is a very effervescent dry beer, not unlike champagne.

HEFE-: A German word meaning "with." Used mostly in conjunction with wheat (weiss) beers to denote that the beer is bottled or kegged with the yeast in suspension (hefe-weiss). These beers are cloudy, frothy, and very refreshing.

HOP: The flowering herb used to flavor and preserve beer. First used in Flanders in the fifteenth century, its use spread rapidly, mainly for its preservative effect on beers that were being shipped long distances.

INDIA PALE ALE: The name given to a high-gravity (7% to 8% alcohol by volume) pale ale that was intentionally well hopped so that it could survive the long voyage from the United Kingdom to the far-reaching military and economic outposts of the British Empire.

KEG: One-half barrel, or 15.5 U.S. gallons.

KRAEUSEN: The addition of fermenting wort to a fermented beer during lagering. The result is a burst of fermentation and an increase in effervescence.

KRIEK: A Belgian lambic beer that has been fermented with ripe cherries in the primary fermentation. The fruit adds a balance to the slightly sour flavor of the lambic.

LAGER: A German word meaning "to store." Used in reference to the storage of bottom fermented beers.

LAMBIC: A beer from the area in and around Bruxelles, Belgium. The fermentation of this malted barley and malted wheat beer is the result of actions of ambient yeast.

LENGTH: The amount of wort brewed each time the brew house is in operation.

LIQUOR: The brewer's word for water used in the brewing process, as included in the mash, or used to sparge the grains after mashing. A traditional phrase used by brewers to differentiate between water and liquor is: "Liquor goes in the beer, water washes the beer off the floor."

MAIBOCK: Traditionally brewed in the spring, this is a strong beer brewed to last in "lager" until the fall. This beer is a traditional beer of Bavaria and is associated with Oktoberfest.

MALT(ING): A process that develops the starch content of grain.

MALT EXTRACT: The condensed wort from a mash, consisting of maltose, dextrins, and other dissolved solids. Either as a syrup or powdered sugar, it is used by brewers, in solutions of water and extract, to reconstitute wort for fermentation.

MALT LIQUOR: A legal term used in the United States to designate a fermented malt beverage of relatively high alcohol content (7% to 8% by volume).

MALTOSE: The sugar derived from mashing barley malt. This sugar is metabolized by yeast to produce beer.

MARZEN: Very close to a Vienna-style beer, these beers are brewed especially for the Oktoberfest held in late September/early October in Munich. These beers are "session" beers that are amber in color and semidry.

MASH: The combination of grist and liquor, heated to a specific temperature for the optimum production of maltose and other nonfermentable products (dextrins).

MICRO-BREWERY: A brewery that produces fewer than 15,000 barrels of beer a year.

MOUTH FEEL: The experience of feeling the body of the beer while tasting it. (*See also* Body.)

OKTOBERFEST: In 1810 the first Oktoberfest was held in Munich's "village green" to celebrate the wedding of Prince Luitpold of Bavaria and his bride, the Bavarian Princess Teressa. It was such a fun wedding that the citizens of Munich have celebrated it every year since (with the exception of only two or three years, when political and military events overshadowed the celebration). Today the green is known as the Theresienwiese (*Wies'n*) and the "March Beer" (brewed in March and tapped for the Oktoberfest) is called "Wies'n Beer."

PALE ALE: A traditional beer brewed in the United Kingdom. This is an amber-colored, very lightly hopped top-fermented brew. The most famous pale ale was, and still is, Bass.

PASTEURIZATION: The heating a liquid to kill spoilage microorganisms, to render it sterile. The process is used on beer to increase the shelf life of the product and stop all fermentation that might still be going on in the solution.

PLZEŇ: The name of a city in the Czech Republic that first began brewing pilsner, the clear, golden bottom-fermented beer. The most famous example of this style of beer is Pilsner Urquell.

PITCHING: A word used to describe the action of adding yeast to a chilled wort in preparation for fermentation.

PORTER: Similar to a stout, but a lighter, less intense beer with a very deep garnet color and a smooth, less astringent flavor than stout. Once a "dead" beer, this style of beer has been reborn, thanks to the micro-breweries in the United States.

RAUCHBIER: A German word (*rauch*/smoke and *bier*/beer) used to describe beer made from malted barley that has been smoked in a way similar to the process used in Scotland to produce smoked grain for the production of Scotch whiskey. A famous rauchbier is produced in the city of Wurtzburg in Franconia, an area in central Germany.

SCOTCH ALE: A strong (6% to 10% alcohol by volume), sweet, full-bodied ale brewed in Scotland. Although this is called an "ale," it is brewed much closer to a lager-style beer: fermented at low temperatures and lagered for up to six months.

SPECIFIC GRAVITY: (*See* GRAVITY.)

STEAM BEER: A beer indigenous to San Francisco in the nineteenth and early twentieth centuries. This is an amber beer, fermented with bottom-fermenting (lager) yeast at relatively high temperatures. Legend has it that the name came from the process of rebunging kegs of the beer. During the process, the fermenting beer would erupt from the bung hole and was called "steam" by the brewers.

STOUT: A name acquired by very dark porter beers. The name was adopted by the Guinness brewing company in Ireland for a dark beer it called "stout porter." In time, the "porter" part of the name was dropped in favor of "stout."

TRAPPIST ALES: These are top-fermented, bottled-conditioned, usually slightly sweet ales brewed by Trappist monks. There are only six true Trappist breweries (five in Belgium and one in the Netherlands): Chimay, Orval, Rochefort, Westmalle, and Sint Sixtus at Westvleteren in Belgium, and Schaapskooi at Koningshoeven in the Netherlands. Only a beer made at a Trappist monastery can officially use the word "Trappist" in the name of its beer.

VIENNA BEER: In the nineteenth century this amber lager beer was the toast of Vienna, Austria. Today, there is only one major brewery producing a Vienna-style beer, and that brewery is in Mexico. The beer is called Dos Equis.

WEISSE: A German word meaning "white" or "wheat," depending on the context. Weissebier is a particular favorite of the Bavarian brewers of Munich. All six of the major breweries in that city brew at least two weisse beers.

WORT: The sweet liquid made up of maltose, liquor, and hop flavoring, which is fermented to make beer.

YEAST: A single-celled fungus of the genus *Saccharomyces.*

Index